NON RETURNUS NON EXCHANGUM

A gift for

_____

From

THIS BOOK WAS CREATED
AND MOSTLY WRITTEN BY
HENRY D. OSTBERG
(HE IS THE ONE TO BLAME!)

The HAPPY BIRTHDAY Gift Book

177 LAUGHS GUARANTEED!

* For details of the guarantee, see page 179

CONTENTS

About this Book

WE ALL KNOW that the easy birthday gift is a tie for a man or a bottle of perfume for a woman.

But I didn't want to do the easy thing. In my eternal quest to please, I found this book — hoping that it will give you a kick.

Sit back. Put on your glasses (or squint, if you're afraid of looking your age). Let *The Happy Birthday Gift Book* make this day something you will remember for minutes to come.

P.S. My personal greetings are expressed on the next few pages.

I am giving you this book because...
(Check one)

☐ Every person should own
at least one book

☐ The Porsche you wanted was
out of stock

☐ You can tear out the first pages
and give this book to someone else

☐ It will make anything else
you get seem terrific by
comparison

☐ You won't be upset when
I forget your birthday
next year

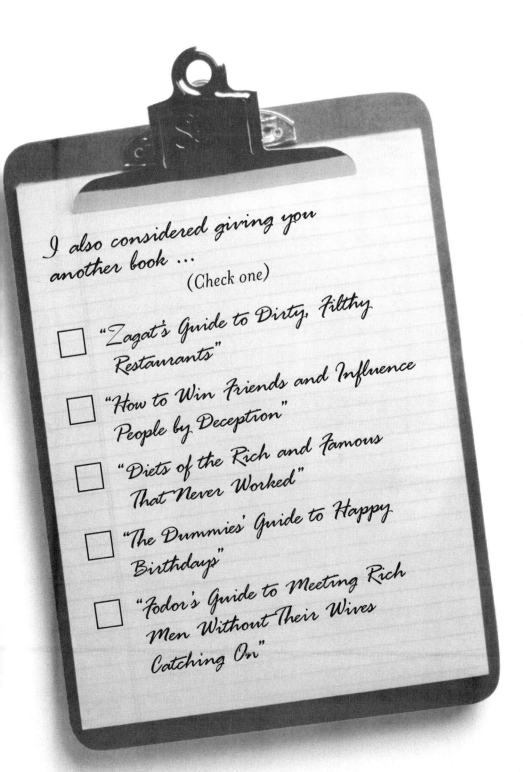

I also considered giving you another book ...

(Check one)

☐ "Zagat's Guide to Dirty, Filthy Restaurants"

☐ "How to Win Friends and Influence People by Deception"

☐ "Diets of the Rich and Famous That Never Worked"

☐ "The Dummies' Guide to Happy Birthdays"

☐ "Fodor's Guide to Meeting Rich Men Without Their Wives Catching On"

If you don't like this book...
(Check one)

☐ Go ahead, bitch and moan

☐ Donate it to the Salvation Army, and take a $10,000 tax deduction

☐ Give it to Al Sharpton, and take a $100,000 tax deduction

☐ Have fun returning shop-lifted merchandise

☐ You **really** won't like what I have decided to give you for Christmas

CHAPTER ONE

It's the Gift
That Counts

SOME CAREFULLY SELECTED GIFTS

FOR YOUR INSURANCE SALESMAN:

A book explaining the meaning of the word "no."

FOR YOUR CONGRESSMAN:

A two-year subscription to *Modern Bribe* magazine.

FOR YOUR ACCOUNTANT:

A set of books ... and another set of books.

FOR YOUR ATTORNEY:

Nothing. He can already buy whatever he wants with your money.

FOR YOUR AUTO MECHANIC:

Membership to the Better Business Bureau.

FOR YOUR DOCTOR:

A warm stethoscope.

ALSO BORN ON THIS DAY IN JANUARY:

1
PAUL REVERE
BETSY ROSS
J. EDGAR HOOVER
FRANK LANGELLA

2
ISAAC ASIMOV
DIANE LANE
CHRISTY TURLINGTON
CUBA GOODING JR.

3
J.R.R. TOLKIEN
VICTOR BORGE
DABNEY COLEMAN
MEL GIBSON

4
LOUIS BRAILLE
FLOYD PATTERSON
DYAN CANNON
JULIA ORMOND

SOME CAREFULLY SELECTED GIFTS

FOR A TEST-TUBE BABY:
A chemistry set. In case he wants to make a little brother.

FOR YOUR PLUMBER:
Extra-large underwear ... to prevent the crack from showing.

FOR YOUR DENTIST:
"Queer Eye" bottled water for rinsing. It swishes all by itself.

FOR YOUR FAVORITE BACHELOR:
The name and telephone number of a sex-starved deaf-mute whose father owns a liquor store.

MORE CAREFULLY SELECTED GIFTS

FOR HER

For the girl who has nothing: *implants.*

For the girl who does nothing: *why bother?*

For the girl who will do anything: *your phone number.*

FOR HIM

For the guy who has everything: *antibiotics.*

For the guy who has nothing: *dinner with the implant girl.*

For the guy who will do nothing: *a psychiatrist.*

JANUARY

10 JIM CROCE
ROD STEWART
GEORGE FOREMAN
PAT BENATAR

11 ALEXANDER
HAMILTON
ROD TAYLOR
NAOMI JUDD
STANLEY TUCCI

12 JOHN HANCOCK
JOHN SINGER
SARGENT
RUSH LIMBAUGH
HOWARD STERN

13 HORATIO ALGER
CHARLES NELSON
REILLY
JULIA LOUIS-DREYFUS
ORLANDO BLOOM

14 BENEDICT ARNOLD
ALBERT SCHWEITZER
ANDY ROONEY
FAYE DUNAWAY

YOU KNOW IT is a CHEAP GIFT if ...

It is tied up with dental floss, instead of a ribbon.

You have something like it ...
and you got it for knocking down three milk bottles.

It comes with a 30-second money-back guarantee.

The person giving it to you asks you sign a non-disclosure agreement.

China's minister of trade calls to make sure you know
it was *not* made in his country.

The label on the box says:
"If accidentally ingested,
don't worry."

15 MOLIÈRE
MARTIN LUTHER
KING JR.
LLOYD BRIDGES
MARIO VAN PEEBLES

16 ETHEL MERMAN
SUSAN SONTAG
SADÉ
KATE MOSS

17 BENJAMIN FRANKLIN
AL CAPONE
MUHAMMED ALI
JIM CARREY

18 DANIEL WEBSTER
OLIVER HARDY
CARY GRANT
KEVIN COSTNER

19 EDGAR ALLEN POE
ROBERT E. LEE
JANIS JOPLIN
DOLLY PARTON

BIRTHDAY GIFT NO-NO'S

Don't try to return a necktie, saying it doesn't fit.

Don't return cash...unless you are sure it is counterfeit
(and only after you have tried to pass it at a bodega).

Don't return a gift certificate, claiming it is the wrong color.

Don't exchange the French impressionist painting you received
for an Albanian one...unless you were born in Albania.

Don't return anything that "fell off the back of a truck"...
unless you want the same thing to happen to you.

JANUARY

20 GEORGE BURNS
FEDERICO FELLINI
"BUZZ" ALDRIN
BILL MAHER

21 BENNY HILL
CHRISTIAN DIOR
TELLY SAVALAS
PLACIDO DOMINGO

22 LORD BYRON
D.W. GRIFFITH
SAM COOKE
LINDA BLAIR

23 JOHN HANCOCK
EDOUARD MANET
CHITA RIVERA
PRINCESS CAROLINE
OF MONACO

24 NEIL DIAMOND
JOHN BELUSHI
NASTASSIA KINSKI
MARY LOU RETTON

THANK YOU CARDS for THOSE GREAT GIFTS

Thank you for the towels.
Hyatt has always been my favorite designer.

Thank you for the first-class airline ticket … on Pan Am.

Thank you for the hideaway couch.
I have already hidden it away in my garage.

Thank you for the box of gourmet foods.
I especially liked the Spam and the Twinkies.

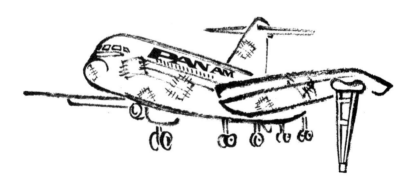

OPENING BIRTHDAY GIFTS WORLDWIDE

IF YOU ARE IN ...

Scotland: Save the wrapping paper.

Sweden: Forget the gift. Find the girl who wrapped it ... and remove *her* wrapping.

Australia: Open a can of Foster's Lager first. After that, *any* gift will seem bloody fantastic.

Uzbekistan: Immediately erase the serial number.

Greenland: Open it very, very slowly ... because there isn't much else to do in Greenland on your birthday.

JANUARY

30 FRANKLIN ROOSEVELT
VANESSA REDGRAVE
GENE HACKMAN
PHIL COLLINS

31 JACKIE ROBINSON
CAROL CHANNING
NORMAN MAILER
JUSTIN TIMBERLAKE

ALSO BORN ON THIS DAY IN FEBRUARY:

1 CLARK GABLE
BORIS YELTSIN
LAURA DERN
LISA MARIE PRESLEY

2 JAMES JOYCE
LIZ SMITH
TOMMY SMOTHERS
FARRAH FAWCETT

IF YOU ARE IN ...

Sicily: Be careful and open the package under water.

Switzerland: If it is a motorcycle, check to make sure it has gears other than neutral.

Finland: Save the ribbon. With six months of total darkness, you may need it to hang yourself.

Germany: Vait fur orders!

— And now —

FOR THOSE OVERWHELMED BY
THE SOPHISTICATED HUMOR
OF THE PREVIOUS PAGES...

FEBRUARY

8 JAMES DEAN JACK LEMON NICK NOLTE JOHN GRISHAM	**9** WILLIAM HENRY HARRISON JOE PESCI CAROLE KING MIA FARROW	**10** JIMMY DURANTE ROBERTA FLACK MARK SPITZ GEORGE STEPHANOPOULIS	**11** THOMAS EDISON BURT REYNOLDS SHERYL CROW JENNIFER ANISTON	**12** ABRAHAM LINCOLN CHARLES DARWIN OMAR BRADLEY ARSENIO HALL

"I hope you kept the receipt!"

"He's celebrating his birthday."

"Have you thought about what you would like
for your birthday?"

CHAPTER TWO

Lights, Camera, Frosting!

BIRTHDAYS of the FAMOUS

ABE LINCOLN:

When he turned 10, Abe Lincoln walked five miles to pick up the gift that his grandmother had sent him. But the post office was closed in honor of his birthday.

GALILEO:

When everyone forgot his 12th birthday, Gailileo threw a tantrum. So his mother yelled, "Whaddya think, the whole world revolves around you?!"

BILL GATES:

On his 13th birthday, Bill Gates got a miniature car. A week later, he called the manufacturer to complain that it kept crashing.

PAMELA ANDERSON:

For her 14th birthday, Pamela Anderson asked her parents for a subscription to *American Gardener* magazine...because she wanted to learn about "flowers and implants."

FEBRUARY	13	14	15	16	17
	CHUCK YEAGER	JACK BENNY	GALILEO GALILEI	EDGAR BERGEN	HAL HOLBROOK
	GEORGE SEGAL	FLORENCE	SUSAN B. ANTHONY	LEVAR BURTON	JIM BROWN
	STOCKARD	HENDERSON	HARVEY KORMAN	JOHN MCENROE	MICHAEL JORDAN
	CHANNING	CARL BERNSTEIN	JANE SEYMOUR	ICE-T	PARIS HILTON
	JERRY SPRINGER	TELLER			

BIRTHDAYS of the FAMOUS

WILLIAM SHAKESPEARE:

Shakespeare suffered a breakdown on his 17th birthday. He found out his mother was being played by a man.

MARIE ANTOINETTE:

On her 25th birthday, Marie Antoinette said, "Let them eat cake. I'm staying on the Atkins diet."

CHARLES LINDBERGH:

Lindbergh made his historic non-stop flight to Paris on his 25th birthday, but had to return the same day, because he had left home without his American Express card.

ALEXANDER GRAHAM BELL:

On his 30th birthday, Alexander Graham Bell got a call from his mother-in-law. So he invented the busy signal.

18	**19**	**20**	**21**	**22**
YOKO ONO	NICOLAS	ANSEL ADAMS	ERMA BOMBECK	GEORGE
JOHN TRAVOLTA	COPERNICUS	SIDNEY POITIER	RUE MCCLANAHAN	WASHINGTON
VANNA WHITE	LEE MARVIN	KELSEY GRAMMER	DAVID GEFFEN	CHICO MARX
MATT DILLON	"MAMA" CASS ELLIOT	CINDY CRAWFORD	TYNE DAILEY	TED KENNEDY
	PRINCE ANDREW			DREW BARRYMORE

BIRTHDAYS of the FAMOUS

NAPOLEON:

Napoleon got an enormous cake on his 31st birthday. "It is much too big," he complained. "All I wanted was a Napoleon."

CHRISTOPHER COLUMBUS:

King Ferdinand told Christopher Columbus on the explorer's 34th birthday: "I've got good news and bad news. There's a beautiful girl being delivered to your room as we speak. But she's flat."

GEORGE WASHINGTON:

On his 48th birthday, George Washington moaned, "It is tough being the first president. I can't blame anything on the prior administration."

| **FEBRUARY** | **23** GEORGE FREDIRIC HANDEL
PETER FONDA
JULIO IGLESIAS
KRISTIN DAVIS | **24** WINSLOW HOMER
ENRICO CARUSO
DOMINIC CHIANESE
PAULA ZAHN | **25** PIERRE-AUGUSTE RENIOR
JIM BACKUS
GEORGE HARRISON
CARROT TOP | **26** VICTOR HUGO
JACKIE GLEASON
TONY RANDALL
JOHNNY CASH | **27** JOHN STEINBECK
JOANNE WOODWARD
ELIZABETH TAYLOR
RALPH NADER |

BIRTHDAYS of the FAMOUS

VINCENT VAN GOGH:
On her 48th birthday, Vincent Van Gogh's girlfriend shrieked, "You schmuck, I said ear - rings!"

RICHARD NIXON:
To celebrate his 61st birthday, Richard Nixon fixed a meal for his 10 best friends. When they all came down with food poisoning, he denied responsibility, saying, "I am not a cook."

DOUGLAS MACARTHUR:
On his 65th birthday, Douglas MacArthur looked at the green polka-dot tie his wife gave him and sighed, "I shall return this."

METHUSELAH:
Buying presents for Methuselah was really tough. What do you give a guy for his 400th birthday?

| **28** MARIO ANDRETTI
TOMMY TUNE
BERNADETTE PETERS
JOHN TURTURRO | **29** JIMMY DORSEY
DINAH SHORE
TONY ROBBINS
JEFF "JA RULE"
ATKINS | **ALSO BORN**
ON THIS DAY IN
MARCH: | **1** GLENN MILLER
DAVID NIVEN
HARRY BELAFONTE
RON HOWARD | **2** DESI ARNAZ
MIKHAIL GORBACHEV
LOU REED
JON BON JOVI |

HOW DIFFERENT PROFESSIONS CELEBRATE

MAFIA WISE GUY:

Cruises up the Hudson River and bobs for Family members.

LAWYER:

Invites guests to bust the piñata . . .

then sues them for damages.

HOLLYWOOD TALENT AGENT:

Serves cake to 80 percent of his guests,

keeping 20 percent for himself.

POSTAL WORKER:

Shows up for his party two weeks late.

MORMON MAN:

Gets depressed. (Who would not be depressed with

more than one mother-in-law?)

MARCH

3 ALEXANDER
   GRAHAM BELL
JEAN HARLOW
MIRANDA
   RICHARDSON
JESSICA BIEL

4 ANTONIO VIVALDI
KNUTE ROCKNEY
JOHN GARFIELD
PATRICIA HEATON

5 JAMES MADISON
REX HARRISON
DEAN STOCKWELL
PENN JILLETTE

6 MICHELANGELO
ED MCMAHON
ROB REINER
SHAQUILLE O'NEAL

7 MAURICE RAVEL
WILLARD SCOTT
TAMMY FAYE
MICHAEL EISNER

HOW DIFFERENT PROFESSIONS CELEBRATE

SKI INSTRUCTOR:

Does not eat the icing on his cake until the conditions are right.

ESKIMO GIRL:

Jumps into the ice-cream cake.

PLUMBER:

Goes to the golf course … and clogs a few holes.

TRANSVESTITE:

Goes to a party to eat, drink and be Mary.

PSYCHIATRIST:

Changes a light bulb
in the office…but only if
the bulb wants to
be changed.

MOVIES to SEE on YOUR BIRTHDAY (but NEVER WILL)

"THE LAST OF THE MOHICANS"

Betty Mohican, proud mother of eight children
conceived on each of her husband's last eight birthdays,
tells her husband she has reached menopause.

"ROMANCING THE STONE"

Feeling romantic, Tipper Gore celebrates her birthday
by trying to make love to Al.

"EMISSION IMPOSSIBLE"

An Arab eunuch, celebrating his 21st birthday,
finds one of the beauties in the sheik's harem extremely attractive
and attempts to make love to her.

"LITTLE CAESAR"

A lawyer, trying to impress his clients, decides to have his birthday party
at the fanciest restaurant in town but, to keep expenses low, tells the
owner to limit the menu to a small salad.

MARCH

13	**14**	**15**	**16**	**17**
L. RON HUBBARD	ALBERT EINSTIEIN	ANDREW JACKSON	JAMES MADISON	NAT "KING" COLE
NEIL SEDAKA	QUINCY JONES	HARRY JAMES	HENNY YOUNGMAN	RUDOLF NUREYEV
WILLIAM H. MACY	MICHAEL CAINE	JUDD HIRSCH	JERRY LEWIS	GARY SINESE
DANA DELANEY	BILLY CRYSTAL	FABIO	ERIK ESTRADA	ROB LOWE

MOVIES to SEE on YOUR BIRTHDAY (but NEVER WILL)

"OCEAN'S 7-ELEVEN"

Danny Ocean, down on his luck after a 10-year prison stint,
invites his associates to celebrate his 50th birthday over a meal of
Yoo-hoo and microwave burritos.

"GONE WITH THE WIND II"

A woman who loves rhubarb invents a product called "Beano"...
to ensure that her few remaining friends come to her birthday party.

"CITIZEN KANE-LESS"

Celebrating his 78th birthday, an old man searches for his cane
so he can go to his surprise party in style.

18 GROVER CLEVELAND	19 WYATT EARP	20 CARL REINER	21 J.S. BACH	22 MARCEL MARCEAU
PETER GRAVES	URSULA ANDRESS	WILLIAM HURT	FLORENZ ZIEGFELD	STEPHEN SONDHEIM
JOHN UPDIKE	GLENN CLOSE	SPIKE LEE	MATTHEW BRODERICK	ANDREW LLOYD
QUEEN LATIFAH	BRUCE WILLIS	HOLLY HUNTER	ROSIE O'DONNELL	WEBBER
				REESE
				WITHERSPOON

BIRTHDAY INS & OUTS

OUT	IN
$100 Wal-Mart gift certificate	$100 cash
Being 39	*Really* being 39
Having a senior moment	Remembering your own cell-phone number
Birthday cake	Atkins low-carb bar
Being rich	Exceeding your credit limit
Your driver's license photo	Your high school yearbook photo
Beer	DeBeers
Food poisoning	Poison perfume, by Dior

MARCH

23 KING LOUIS XIV
JUAN GRIS
JOAN CRAWFORD
CHAKA KHAN

24 HARRY HOUDINI
STEVE MCQUEEN
BOB MACKIE
LOUIE ANDERSON

25 ARTURO TOSCANINI
ARETHA FRANKLIN
ELTON JOHN
SARAH JESSICA
PARKER

26 TENNESSEE
WILLIAMS
SANDRA DAY
O'CONNOR
DIANA ROSS
BOB WOODWARD

27 GLORIA SWANSON
SARAH VAUGHAN
QUENTIN TARANTINO
MARIAH CAREY

BIRTHDAY LOGIC

On his 34th birthday, a wife tried to dissuade her husband from drinking in the future. She went to a fishing-equipment store and bought some worms. Returning home, she got two shot glasses, filling one with water and the other with whiskey.

Asking her husband to come to the table, she said, "I want you to see this." She put a worm in the glass with water; the worm swam around. She put the other worm in the glass with whiskey; that worm died immediately.

Feeling that she had made her point, she said, "What do you have to say about this experiment?"

His answer was prompt: "If I drink whiskey, I won't get worms."

LET'S PLAY JEO-PARTY!

ANSWER: Return a birthday gift to Kmart.

QUESTION: How do you get change for a parking meter?

ANSWER: The parents.

QUESTION: Who cries most at a gay birthday party?

ANSWER: Britney Spears, Donald Trump and upside-down.

QUESTION: Name a flake, a snake and a cake.

ANSWER: Jump out of a birthday cake wearing a bikini.

QUESTION: What is the last thing you ever want to see your father do?

ANSWER: Siamese twins.

QUESTION: Who are always together on their birthday?

LET'S PLAY JEO-PARTY!

ANSWER: Antibiotics.

QUESTION: What is the door prize at a hooker's birthday party?

ANSWER: Spin the bottle and strip poker.

QUESTION: Name two games you hope no one plays at RuPaul's birthday party.*

*For those who live in a cave without television, she is really a he.

6	7	8	9	10
BUTCH CASSIDY	WALTER WINCHELL	BUDDHA	PAUL ROBESON	JOSEPH PULITZER
ANDRÉ PREVIN	BILLIE HOLIDAY	MARY PICKFORD	HUGH HEFNER	OMAR SHARIF
BILLY DEE WILLIAMS	FRANCIS FORD	JACQUES BREL	DENNIS QUAID	DON MEREDITH
MARILU HENNER	COPPOLA	KOFI ANNAN	CYNTHIA NIXON	STEVEN SEAGAL
	RUSSELL CROWE			

RULES to GROW OLD BY

Don't drink and drive. You might hit a bump and spill your drink.

If at first you don't succeed, change the rules.

It doesn't matter whether you win or lose.
What really counts is whom you blame.

A bird in the hand ... is something you should never have
during a job interview.

RULES to GROW OLD BY

There is no such thing as a free lunch …
unless you find a cockroach in your tuna melt.

If you can't beat'm, they are the
wrong crowd for your next S&M
party.

When life gives you lemons,
add a shot of vodka.

When you are sick, stay the hell away from anyone you care about.

16	**17**	**18**	**19**	**20**
WILBUR WRIGHT CHARLIE CHAPLIN KAREEM ABDUL JABBAR MARTIN LAWRENCE	THORNTON WILDER NIKITA KHRUSHCHEV WILLIAM HOLDEN JENNIFER GARNER	CLARENCE DARROW JAMES WOODS ERIC MCCORMACK CONAN O'BRIEN	DUDLEY MOORE DON ADAMS ASHLEY JUDD KATE HUDSON	RYAN O'NEAL JESSICA LANGE LUTHER VANDROSS CARMEN ELECTRA

～ And now ～

A FEW WORDS
FROM AN OTHERWISE UNEMPLOYED
CARTOONIST...

"Staying fit as we got older sure paid off."

"Here it is my birthday...and not one card!"

"That's so sweet. A birthday card
from an online collection agency."

CHAPTER THREE

Looking Back

THE EARLY YEARS

SOME PEOPLE HAVE A TOUGH TIME GROWING UP.
THERE IS THIS FELLOW WHO...

Received a pack of cigarettes from his father
for his third birthday. His mother said he
could smoke...but only in bed.

When he turned 10, he did not
want to get any older.
He was afraid that he would have to
grow more fingers.

He never had a 13th birthday.
His father was an elevator operator, so he made him skip it.

He wanted to play hide-and-seek at his 14th birthday party . . .
but nobody wanted to seek him.

APRIL

26 JOHN JAMES AUDUBON
COUNT BASIE
IM PEI
CAROL BURNETT

27 ULYSSES S. GRANT
SAMUEL MORSE
JACK KLUGMAN
CASEY KASEM

28 JAMES MONROE
LIONEL BARRYMORE
ANN-MARGRET
JAY LENO

29 DUKE ELLINGTON
JERRY SEINFELD
UMA THURMAN
ANDRE AGASSI

30 WILLIE NELSON
CLORIS LEACHMAN
JILL CLAYBURGH
KIRSTEN DUNST

THE LATER YEARS

As he grew older, things got worse. . .

For his 15th birthday, he asked his parents for a bigger bedroom. They removed the wallpaper.

He wanted to play post office at his 16th birthday party. But the girls did not like his looks, so they insisted it was a federal holiday.

On his 27th birthday, his wife told him, "A man is like a good wine. He gets better with age." Then she locked him in the cellar.

Last year, his friends threw him a real surprise party. They invited only people to whom he owed money.

He was born in a leap year. He is not allowed to drink until he is 84.

BORN TOO RICH

SOME PEOPLE ARE MORE FORTUNATE.
THERE WAS THIS LUCKY SOUL WHO WAS BORN SO RICH THAT ...

His maternity ward was the presidential suite at the Waldorf-Astoria.

His baby teeth were insured by Lloyd's of London.

He had a French nanny ... named Catherine Deneuve.

He wore Givenchy diapers ... with
Cartier diaper pins.

His playpen contained a full-sized
tennis court.

 MAY

| 5 | KARL MARX SPENCER TRACY TYRONE POWER MARY ASTOR | 6 | SIGMUND FREUD ORSON WELLS WILLIE MAYS GEORGE CLOONEY | 7 | TCHAIKOVSKY EVA PERON GARY COOPER TIM RUSSERT | 8 | HARRY S. TRUMAN DON RICKLES RICKY NELSON ENRIQUE INGLESIAS | 9 | MIKE WALLACE ALBERT FINNEY CANDICE BERGEN BILLY JOEL |

BORN TOO RICH

He learned to walk by changing planes in Geneva
on his way to kindergarten.

For his fifth birthday, he asked his father for something small.
He got Rhode Island.

For his seventh birthday, he asked his father for a sandbox.
He got Yemen.

10 FRED ASTAIR
NANCY WALKER
SID VICIOUS
BONO

11 IRVING BERLIN
SALVADOR DALI
MORT SAHL
NATASHA
RICHARDSON

12 FLORENCE
NIGHTINGALE
KATHERINE HEPBURN
BURT BACHARACH
GEORGE CARLIN

13 JOE LOUIS
BEATRICE ARTHUR
HARVERY KEITEL
STEVIE WONDER

14 BOBBY DARIN
GEORGE LUCAS
TIM ROTH
CATE BLANCHETT

BORN TOO POOR

BUT PITY THE POOR GUY WHO WAS BORN SO POOR THAT ...

The doctor insisted on delivering him C.O.D.

He learned to speak by shouting to
creditors through the front door, "Nobody's home!"

At his sixth birthday party, a social worker jumped out of his cake.

At his eighth birthday party,
the guests played pin the tail on the rodent.

 MAY

15 FLORENCE
NIGHTINGALE
JAMES MASON
RICHARD AVEDON
MADELINE ALBRIGHT

16 HENRY FONDA
LIBERACE
PIERCE BROSNAN
JANET JACKSON

17 DENNIS HOPPER
SUGAR RAY LEONARD
BILL PAXTON
BOB SAGET

18 FRANK CAPRA
PERRY COMO
POPE JOHN PAUL II
REGGIE JACKSON

19 MALCOLM X
DAVID HARTMAN
PETE TOWNSHEND
NORA EPHRON

BORN TOO POOR

At the maternity ward, his father gave out cigarette butts …
instead of cigars.

His parents could only afford to send him to summer camp
in the off-season.

On Halloween, the other kids in the neighborhood
dressed up to look like him.

— ~ **And now** ~ —

FOR THE REAL REASON

SOMEONE GAVE YOU THIS BOOK...

———

MAY

25 MILES DAVIS
BEVERLY SILLS
IAN MCKELLEN
MIKE MYERS

26 AL JOLSON
JOHN WAYNE
STEVIE NICKS
LENNY KRAVITZ

27 WILD BILL HICKOCK
DASHIELL HAMMETT
VINCENT PRICE
HENRY KISSINGER

28 JIM THORPE
IAN FLEMING
GLADYS KNIGHT
RUDOLPH GIULIANI

29 PATRICK HENRY
BOB HOPE
JOHN F. KENNEDY
ANNETTE BENING

"For your father's birthday, we're going back to Woodstock.
Can you score us some weed?"

"Just once, can't you leave your work at the office?"

"I don't think my wife trusts me. When I gave her a check
for her birthday, she insisted that it be certified."

CHAPTER FOUR

You Are Not Getting Older (Only Better)

THE GOLDEN LEERS

Filling out a credit application, a woman hesitated
when it came to stating her age. The clerk behind the window smiled
and said, "The longer you wait, the worse it gets."

A rich hillbilly died at 65 years of age and
left all his money to his wife.
The problem is, she can't touch it until she is 15 years old.

A 60-year-old man saw a cute 20-year-old girl in a bar.
He asked her: "Where have you been all my life?"
She said "Teething."

On his 72nd birthday, a man started walking
three miles a day. By the time he was 80,
his family didn't know where the hell he was.

MAY

30 PETER THE GREAT
BENNY GOODMAN
MEL BLANC
WYNONNA JUDD

31 CLINT EASTWOOD
JOE NAMATH
BROOKE SHIELDS
COLIN FARRELL

ALSO BORN
ON THIS DAY IN
JUNE:

1 MARILYN MONROE
ANDY GRIFFITH
PAT BOONE
MORGAN FREEMAN

2 MARQUIS DE SADE
THOMAS HARDY
JOHNNY
  WEISSMULLER
MARVIN HAMLISH

THE GOLDEN LEERS

A 75-year-old man went to the doctor to complain
that his love life was slowing down.
When the doctor asked him when he noticed it first, the man replied
"Twice last night and again this morning."

An 80-year-old man told his doctor:
"Next week, I'm marrying a 21-year old girl."
The doctor said, "That could be fatal."
The man replied "If she has to die, she has to die."

A man knows he is getting old
when he can only chase girls
downhill.

THE GOLDEN LEERS

On his 65th birthday, a man was told by his doctor
that he had a few hours to live. He immediately returned home,
informed his wife, and said, "Let's make love until dawn."
"That's easy for you to say," she replied.
"You won't have to get up in the morning."

A man of 90 can keep his youth for years …
if he gives her diamonds and furs frequently.

A man is as young as the women he feels.

CHANGING TIMES

When a man is young, he carries condoms in his pocket.
When he gets older, he carries Tums.
That's because he knows he is going to get heartburn ...
before he has sex.

When she was young,
she carried a picture of Rudolph Valentino in her purse.
Now, she carries a picture of Rudolph Giuliani...
to scare off the terrorists.

A FEMALE PERSPECTIVE

The best 10 years of a woman's life are between 28 and 30.

A woman's age is like an odometer on a used car.
You know it has been set back. You just don't know how far.

The five ages of women are: childhood, teens,
young woman, young woman and young woman.

There is one sure way to find out a woman's age.
Ask her mother-in-law.

JUNE

18 EG MARSHALL
PAUL MCCARTNEY
ROGER EBERT
ISABELLA ROSSELLNI

19 LOU GEHRIG
GUY LOMBARDO
KATHLEEN TURNER
PAULA ABDUL

20 DANNY AIELLO
LIONEL RICHIE
JOHN GOODMAN
NICOLE KIDMAN

21 AL HIRSCHFELD
JUDY HOLLIDAY
JANE RUSSELL
PRINCE WILLIAM

22 BILLY WILDER
KRIS KRISTOFFERSON
MERYL STREEP
CYNDI LAUPER

A FEMALE PERSPECTIVE

A woman never forgets her age, once she decides what it is.

Age creeps up on a woman.
Especially when she marries an older man.

The best way to tell a woman's age is when she is not around.

A woman knows she is getting old
when she goes to the beauty parlor
... just to get an estimate.

YOU KNOW YOU ARE GETTING OLD IF ...

You remember championship boxing matches
between two white guys.

All the numbers in your little black book are doctors.

You want a calendar with big numbers,
rather than one showing girls with big breasts.

You smoke after sex.
And one pack lasts you a whole year.

Your idea of a hot night
is to crank up the electric blanket on your bed.

You have to pay for sex ... and get a refund.

| JUNE | 28 | KING HENRY VIII
MEL BROOKS
KATHY BATES
JOHN CUSACK | 29 | NELSON EDDY
GARY BUSEY
RICHARD LEWIS
FRED GRANDY | 30 | BUDDY RICH
WILLIE SUTTON
LENA HORNE
MIKE TYSON | ALSO BORN
ON THIS DAY IN
JULY: | 1 | SYDNEY POLLACK
DAN AYKROYD
DEBORAH HARRY
PRINCESS DIANA |

YOU KNOW YOU ARE GETTING OLD IF ...

You order a three-minute egg and the waitress asks
for payment up front.

You turn out the lights to save on the electric bill, not for romance.

Gypsy fortune-tellers refuse your business.

Your idea of
a quickie is getting
pick-pocketed.

You feel your corns
more than your oats.

YOU KNOW YOU ARE GETTING OLD IF ...

You spend more time looking at the menu than at the waitress.

It takes you all night to do what you used to do all night.

You go to the barber once a month, just to reminisce.

Your birthday makes front-page news ...
though most people have never heard of you.

YOU KNOW YOU ARE GETTING OLD IF ...

You get a letter from a nursing home, marked "URGENT."

Peeping Toms call and ask you to close your drapes.

You sink your teeth into a steak and they stay there.

You go into the hospital for a transfusion ...
only to be told that your blood type has been discontinued.

You take up jogging, just to hear heavy breathing.

Your doctor asks you *not* to cough ...
to conserve your strength.

12	13	14	15	16
MILTON BERLE	PATRICK STEWART	WOODY GUTHRIE	REMBRANDT	MARY BAKER EDDY
BILL COSBY	HARRISON FORD	GERALD FORD	VAN RIJN	GINGER ROGERS
RICHARD SIMMONS	CHEECH MARIN	ARTHUR LAURENTS	LINDA RONSTADT	ORVILLE
CHERYL LADD	PAUL PRUDHOMME	INGMAR BERGMAN	JESSE VENTURA	REDENBACHER
			KIM ALEXIS	WILL FERRELL

HE IS SO OLD THAT ...

His Social Security number is 000-00-00011.

When he was in school, there were no history classes.

His life-insurance policy is signed by John Hancock personally.

When he went in for a physical checkup,
the doctor recommended a carbon-14 test.

He is hard of hearing from the Big Bang.

He took driver's ed in a stagecoach.

 JULY

17	18	19	20	21
JAMES CAGNEY PHYLLIS DILLER DIHANN CARROLL DONALD SUTHERLAND	RED SKELTON NELSON MANDELA JOHN GLENN VIN DIESEL	EDGAR DEGAS LIZZIE BORDEN GEORGE HAMILTON VIKKI CARR	SIR EDMUND HILLARY NATALIE WOOD DIANA RIGG CARLOS SANTANA	ERNEST HEMINGWAY ISAAC STERN ROBIN WILLIAMS JOSH HARTNETT

HE IS SO OLD THAT ...

He remembers the Dead Sea when it was only feeling sick.

People complement him on his alligator shoes ...
when he's barefoot.

His birth certificate contains the word "circa."

His birthstone is molten lava.

THE ULTIMATE BIRTHDAY PRESENT

On his 40th birthday, a man went to a Rolls Royce dealer and told him he wanted the very best model, fully loaded.

When the car was delivered a few weeks later, he drove it around town. To his amazement, he saw another man driving the same model. At a stoplight, he asked him how he liked his car. The man said, "It is terrific. Especially the vibrating bed in the back."

Angry that he did not have the same option, he went back to his dealer and demanded that a vibrating bed be installed.

A few weeks later, he encountered the same man in the other Rolls Royce. He lowered his window to talk to him, but there was no response. So he beeped his horn, but still nothing. Then he beeped again.

Finally, the other owner lowered his window and bellowed, "How dare you disturb me when I'm in my sauna!"

THE GREAT HEREAFTER

O n his 72nd birthday, Sam was driving home from his favorite restaurant when he and his wife met their demise in a crash.

Arriving in heaven, they were escorted to a sprawling, beautifully-furn- shed mansion.

"Welcome to your new home," an angel told them.

When Sam asked how much the place cost, the angel said, "Nothing. This is your reward for being good people."

Looking out the window, Sam saw a championship golf course.

"What are the green fees?" he asked.

The angel replied, "Nothing — you can play for free every day."

Then the angel took the couple to a lavish buffet lunch. "Eat as much as you want. It's all free for you to enjoy," he said.

So Sam asked, "Where are the low-fat and low-calorie foods?"

"Don't worry — this is heaven," the angel responded. "You can eat what- ever you want."

But Sam persisted. "Where's the gym?" he asked.

"No need to work out in heaven," the angel said. "No matter how much you eat, you will never gain an ounce."

At that point, Sam glared at his wife and said, "You and your damn bran muffins. We could have been here 15 years ago!"

ALSO BORN
ON THIS DAY IN
AUGUST:

1	2	3	4
HERMAN MELVILLE	JAMES BALDWIN	ANNE KLEIN	LOUIS ARMSTRONG
YVES ST. LAURENT	CARROLL O'CONNOR	TONY BENNETT	HELEN THOMAS
JERRY GARCIA	PETER O'TOOLE	MARTIN SHEEN	RICHARD BELZER
DOM DELUISE	WES CRAVEN	MARTHA STEWART	BILLY BOB THORNTON

— **And now** —

FOR THOSE WHO THINK

COLORING CARTOONS CAN BE FUN...

"Aftershave! Wow! Just what I needed."

"What birthday gift can you suggest for a woman
who wants everything?"

"How do you expect me to remember your birthday when
you never look any older?"

CHAPTER FIVE

Party Time

TOP TEN REASONS TO CELEBRATE YOUR BIRTHDAY

10. If you had not been born, you would never have received this spectacular book.

9. It is a good reason to put on clean underwear.

8. If your birthday is a dud, imagine what the day would have been like if it were not your birthday.

7. If you usually lie about your age, now you can tell a "whopper."

6. Stop blaming your parents for your good looks, great personality and trust fund. Suffering makes you a better person.

5. Be glad that birthdays come only once a year.

4. You probably gave cheap presents to friends in the past, so this is their time to get even.

3. You get to blow your germs all over a cake...then watch people gobble it up.

2. Try to forget you're one day closer to a face-lift.

1. It is time you stopped believing you were delivered by the stork.

AUGUST

10 HERBERT HOOVER / EDDIE FISHER / JIMMY DEAN / ANTONIO BANDERAS

11 ALEX HALEY / MIKE DOUGLAS / JERRY FALWELL / "HULK" HOGAN

12 CECIL B. DEMILLE / GEORGE SOROS / GEORGE HAMILTON / PETE SAMPRAS

13 ANNIE OAKLEY / BERT LAHR / ALFRED HITCHCOCK / DON HO

14 DANIELLE STEELE / RUSSELL BAKER / STEVE MARTIN / HALLE BERRY

JOIN THE PARTY

There are two types of guests at a birthday party:
one who wants to leave early and one who wants to stay late.
The problem is…they are usually married to each other.

A guest said to the hostess,
"I've noticed your husband is serving liquor,
but he doesn't drink a drop himself."
The hostess replied, "We have a rule against him drinking
at his birthday party. When he does, he gets loaded…
and brings out the good stuff."

At the end of a modest birthday celebration,
one of the guests told the hostess,
"We hate to eat and run, but my husband is still hungry."

THINGS NOT TO DO WHEN ARRIVING AT YOUR OWN SURPRISE PARTY

If it is at your house, do not ring the doorbell.

Do not walk in with a camera.

If you usually wear a toupee, keep it in your pocket.

If you are a lawyer, look happy.

If you are an accountant, look alive.

THINGS NOT TO SAY WHEN ARRIVING AT YOUR OWN SURPRISE PARTY

"A surprise party — wow!
It's good I wore my tux to work this morning."

"Sorry I'm late, but I had to pick up extra balloons
and cocktail wieners."

"If anyone wants to give cash instead of a gift,
I can change fifties, hundreds...whatever you got."

"Six people...that's it? I had at least 50 on the guest list."

"Where the hell are the strippers? I booked them for 8:30!"

---

25 LEONARD BERNSTEIN
MONTY HALL
SEAN CONNERY
REGIS PHILBIN

26 CHRISTOPHER
COLUMBUS
BEN BRADLEE
GERALDINE FERRARO
MACAULAY CULKIN

27 CONFUCIUS
LYNDON B. JOHNSON
MOTHER TERESA
BARBARA BACH

28 JOHANN VON
GOETHE
LEO TOLSTOY
JASON PRIESTLEY
SHANIA TWAIN

29 INGRID BERGMAN
CHARLIE "BIRD"
PARKER
ELLIOTT GOULD
MICHAEL JACKSON

CELEBRITIES SEND THEIR REGRETS

PARIS HILTON:

"I'm tied up in my new video."

ANGELINA JOLIE:

"Oops! Had the wrong date tattooed on my arm."

SIMON COWELL:

"I regret not being able to attend. I also regret that you are
so bloody untalented, stupid and ugly."

JAMES GANDOLFINI:

"Can't be there because a business associate is dying …
next Wednesday at 3 a.m."

STEPHEN KING:

"Will miss being there! Would love to have seen the girl
coming out of the cake I sent … one limb at a time."

AUGUST

30 SHIRLEY BOOTH
FRED MACMURRAY
WARREN BUFFETT
CAMERON DIAZ

31 BUDDY HACKETT
ITZHAK PERLMAN
RICHARD GERE
CHRIS TUCKER

ALSO BORN
ON THIS DAY IN
SEPTEMBER:

1 ROCKY MARCIANO
LILY TOMLIN
BARRY GIBB
DR. PHIL MCGRAW

2 JIMMY CONNORS
MARK HARMON
KEANU REEVES
SALMA HAYEK

CELEBRITIES SEND THEIR REGRETS

COLIN FARRELL:

"I'm stuck in Georgia. Georgia also sends her regrets."

JOAN RIVERS:

"Can't be there. But when you blow out your candles,
wish for a nose job. The lipo can wait."

DAVID BLAINE:

"I'm performing in China that week.
But who says I can't be in two places at once?"

YOUR BIRTHDAY PARTY IS OVER WHEN ...

The music gets so loud that neighbors phone in their requests.

The Red Cross shows up with coffee and blankets.

The most requested drink is Alka-Seltzer.

It is time for a second shave.

You are dancing to the rhythm of the vacuum cleaner.

YOUR BIRTHDAY PARTY IS OVER WHEN ...

The hostess appears in a nightgown.

The sun comes up for the second time.

Someone passes you the rent envelope.

AT YOUR BIRTHDAY PARTY,
YOU HAVE HAD TOO MUCH to DRINK IF ...

You forget the words to "Happy Birthday."

You ask a pregnant guest if you can kiss the baby.

A mosquito bites you, then flies into the wall.

Guests ask you not to breathe near the candles.

The bottle is standing still ... and you are spinning.

You ask the host not to blink her eyes so loudly.

You keep asking for ice cubes on the rocks.

SEPTEMBER

18 GRETA GARBO
FRANKIE AVALON
JAMES GANDOLFINI
LANCE ARMSTRONG

19 WILLIAM GOLDING
TWIGGY
JEREMY IRONS
JIMMY FALLON

20 UPTON SINCLAIR
DR. JOYCE BROTHERS
ANNE MEARA
SOPHIA LOREN

21 STEPHEN KING
BILL MURRAY
RICKI LAKE
FAITH HILL

22 JOHN HOUSEMAN
TOMMY LASORDA
DEBBY BOONE
ANDREA BOCELLI

AT YOUR BIRTHDAY PARTY, YOU HAVE HAD TOO MUCH to DRINK IF ...

A girl jumps out of your cake ...

and you call the cops.

You make a pass at your wife.

Your wife serves you a piece of cake

and you tip her.

You tip her more than 15 percent.

You start unwrapping your guests.

The hostess asks you to leave ...

and it is your own house.

23 MICKEY ROONEY
RAY CHARLES
BRUCE SPRINGSTEEN
JASON ALEXANDER

24 F. SCOTT FITZGERALD
JIM MCKAY
ANTHONY NEWLEY
JIM HENSON

25 BARBARA WALTERS
MICHAEL DOUGLAS
CHRISTOPHER
REEVE
CATHERINE
ZETA-JONES

26 GEORGE GERSHWIN
OLIVIA
NEWTON-JOHN
JAMES CAVIEZEL
SERENA WILLIAMS

27 SAMUEL ADAMS
JAYNE MEADOWS
MEATLOAF
AVRIL LAVIGNE

HOW TO HINT THE PARTY IS OVER

Turn off the rock 'n' roll records,
and play a Vienese waltz.

Ask someone to go out and
pick up the morning paper.

Go to the nearest mirror and put cold cream on your face.

Start writing checks for the
catered food and liquor you ordered.

Play a game:
ask everyone to put on their overcoats,
offering a prize to the person who does it the fastest.

DRESSING TIPS FOR THE LADIES

Remember: a man hates to see a woman in cheap clothing
at a birthday party ... unless it is his wife.

If the shoes you are wearing fit, they are out of style.

Lampshades are acceptable headwear only after midnight.

If wearing a fur coat to the birthday party,
don't worry about how many animals
were killed to make it ...
just think about how many
you had to sleep with to get it.

Never wear the same dress as the birthday girl ...
especially if you are a man.

YOU SPENT TOO LITTLE on YOUR CHILD'S BIRTHDAY PARTY IF ...

The invitation says "BYOB" ... "bring your own balloons."

Instead of pulling a rabbit out of it,
the magician passes his hat among the kids.

After his performance,
the clown asks you to sign his community-service voucher.

The guest of honor plays
"eenie meenie miney mo"
to determine who gets the other
Hostess Cupcake.

There is no piñata.
The kids are told to beat a tree
until something falls out.

OCTOBER

7
DESMOND TUTU
OLIVER NORTH
YO-YO MA
SIMON COWELL

8
JESSE JACKSON
CHEVY CHASE
SIGOURNEY WEAVER
MATT DAMON

9
JOHN LENNON
JACKSON BROWNE
ROBERT WUHL
TONY SHALHOUB

10
GIUSEPPE VERDI
HELEN HAYES
BEN VEREEN
DAVID LEE ROTH

11
ELEANOR ROOSEVELT
JEROME ROBBINS
RON LEIBMAN
LUKE PERRY

YOU SPENT TOO MUCH on YOUR CHILD'S BIRTHDAY PARTY IF ...

The birthday cake arrives in a Brinks truck.

You tried to hire David Letterman
as the emcee ... and he sent you his
top ten reasons why he can't come.

You arrange for the kids to have
pony rides at Churchill Downs.

Your child faints after trying to
blow out the *neon* candles on his cake.

Each guest leaves with two balloons:
a small one on a string
and a big one to take around the world in eighty days.

— And now —

FOR THOSE WHO DEMAND
SHORT PUNCH LINES...

OCTOBER

17 ARTHUR MILLER
RITA HAYWORTH
EVEL KNIEVEL
EMINEM

18 CHUCK BERRY
PETER BOYLE
JEAN-CLAUDE VAN
DAMME
WYNTON MARSALIS

19 JOHN LE CARRÉ
JACK ANDERSON
PETER MAX
JOHN LITHGOW

20 BELA LUGOSI
ART BUCHWALD
KEITH HERNANDEZ
SNOOP DOGG

21 ALFRED NOBEL
DIZZY GILLESPIE
JUDGE JUDY
CARRIE FISHER

"It's a thank you note...
for the birthday gift we sent your brother."

"I guess we'll open the presents later."

"I wrote something loving in this card to my wife.
Before I sign it, run it by legal."

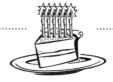

CHAPTER SIX

Thoughts to Cherish

STOP to THINK

Count your life by smiles, not tears.
Count your age by friends, not years.

Age doesn't matter ... if your matter doesn't age.

Don't worry about avoiding temptation.
As you grow older, it will avoid you.

Inside every older person is a younger person ...
wondering what the hell happened.

There are two ways to keep from getting old: lie about your age ...
or drink while driving.

OCTOBER

22 CATHERINE
    DENEUVE
DEREK JACOBI
TONY ROBERTS
JEFF GOLDBLUM

23 JOHNNY CARSON
    PELÉ
MICHAEL CRICHTON
WEIRD AL
    YANKOVIC

24 JACK L. WARNER
    MOSS HART
F. MURRAY
    ABRAHAM
KEVIN KLINE

25 GEORGES BIZET
PABLO PICASSO
MINNIE PEARL
HELEN REDDY

26 BOB HOSKINS
PAT SAJAK
JACLYN SMITH
HILLARY CLINTON

STOP to THINK

I am too wise to want to be younger again.

Remember, it is better to be over the hill than under it.

Also remember that age is unimportant ... unless you're a cheese.

Sixty-five is a terrific birthday ... if you hate your job.

I pray that I may live each day as though it were my last.
I pray that I may live my life as though it were everlasting.

At 85, you stop caring about the birthday presents you will get.
You care about waking up.

27 CAPT. JAMES COOK	28 JONAS SALK	29 FANNY BRICE	30 JOHN ADAMS	31 DAN RATHER
THEODORE ROOSEVELT	DENNIS FRANZ	RICHARD DREYFUSS	FYODOR DOSTOEVSKY	MICHAEL LANDON
SYLVIA PLATH	BILL GATES	KATE JACKSON	HENRY WINKLER	JOHN CANDY
JOHN CLEESE	JULIA ROBERTS	WINONA RYDER	HARRY HAMLIN	JANE PAULEY

WORDS from the WISE

Despite all the advances in medicine,
there is still no cure for the common birthday.
— John Glenn

Old age is fifteen years older than whatever you are.
— Oliver Wendell Holmes

There are three ages of man: youth, middle age and
"Gee, you look really good."
— Red Skelton

Marriage is the alliance of two people,
one of whom never remembers birthdays and the other
who never forgets them.
— Ogden Nash

NOVEMBER

**ALSO BORN
ON THIS DAY IN
NOVEMBER:**

1
STEPHEN CRANE
LYLE LOVETT
JEFF PROBST
JENNY MCCARTHY

2
JAMES K. POLK
DANIEL BOONE
WARREN G.
  HARDING
BURT LANCASTER

3
CHARLES BRONSON
LULU
ROSEANNE BARR
DENNIS MILLER

4
WILL ROGERS
WALTER CRONKITE
DORIS ROBERTS
SEAN "P. DIDDY"
  COMBS

WORDS from the WISE: FOR the LADIES

It's sad to grow old, but nice to ripen.
— Brigitte Bardot

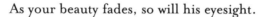

Marry a man your own age.
As your beauty fades, so will his eyesight.
— Phyllis Diller

I've got everything I had 20 years ago, except now it's all lower.
— Gypsy Rose Lee

I was born in 1962. It's true.
And the room next to me was 1963.
—Joan Rivers

— And now —

THE REASON YOU SHOULD
TREASURE THIS BOOK...
AND NOT STORE IT IN THE BATHROOM...

NOVEMBER

10 RICHARD BURTON
ROY SCHEIDER
SINBAD
MACKENZIE
PHILLIPS

11 GEORGE PATTON
DEMI MOORE
CALISTA FLOCKHART
LEONARDO
DICAPRIO

12 AUGUSTE RODIN
GRACE KELLY
NEIL YOUNG
DAVID SCHWIMMER

13 ROBERT LOUIS
STEVENSON
JOE MANTEGNA
WHOOPI GOLDBERG
CHRIS NOTH

14 ROBERT FULTON
CLAUDE MONET
PRINCE CHARLES
LAURA SAN
GIACOMO

"I'm so excited! My boyfriend says he has something special to tell me for my birthday—and he wants to do it on the Jerry Springer show."

"I want to return this birthday gift.
I'm tapered the other way."

"My wife's favorite position
is facing Bloomingdale's."

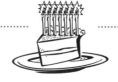

CHAPTER SEVEN

Heavens Forbid!

Aries

March 20 - April 18

WHAT THE STARS SAY...

Aries, the ram, is a sign of people who are self-confident and like to stand out from the crowd. Ruled by the planet Mars, they are shrewd, direct and like to get to the heart of a matter. They can also be skeptical and selfish.

THOSE WHO KNOW YOU ADD...

- Being ruled by Mars, to say nothing of Mounds and M&M's, you should ease up on the sweets...before a planet is named after you.

- You exude complete confidence. You fill out crossword puzzles with a fountain pen.

- Your shrewdness is always evident. Seeing girls dancing on their toes at a ballet, you immediately asked, "Why don't they just get taller girls?"

- Skeptic that you are, you do not believe everything you hear . . . but you don't hesitate to repeat it.

Taurus
April 19 - May 20

WHAT THE STARS SAY...

Taurus, the bull, stands for reliability and determination. Being realists, those born under this sign often seek material possessions to show their achievements. They can also be vain and overly cautious.

THOSE WHO KNOW YOU ADD...

- As a realist, you have known for many years that there is no Santa Claus...because the Tooth Fairy told you so.

- Your determination consistently shows. When at first you do not succeed, you destroy the evidence that you ever tried.

- Being cautious, you hate to make quick decisions.
  When taking a wedding vow, you would say "We will see."

- Because of your vanity, you recently requested your doctor to "touch up" your x-ray.

20	**21**	**22**	**23**	**24**
ALISTAIR COOKE	VOLTAIRE	HOAGY CARMICHAEL	FRANKLIN PIERCE	ZACHARY TAYLOR
ROBERT KENNEDY	MARLO THOMAS	RODNEY	BILLY THE KID	TOULOUSE-LAUTREC
DICK SMOTHERS	GOLDIE HAWN	DANGERFIELD	HARPO MARX	SCOTT JOPLIN
BO DEREK	HAROLD RAMIS	BILLIE JEAN KING	STEVE HARVEY	WILLIAM F. BUCKLEY
		JAMIE LEE CURTIS		

Gemini

May 21 - June 20

WHAT THE STARS SAY...

Gemini, the twins, represents people who are versatile, with a strong desire to master new skills. They tend to be communicative and enthusiastic. They can also be restless and superficial, though they are never boring in bed.

THOSE WHO KNOW YOU ADD...

- In your versatility and quest for new skills, you have decided to learn cross-country skiing ... but you are going to start with a small country.

- You have your wits about you. You know for sure that Taco Bell is really the Mexican telephone company.

- Your enthusiasm knows no bounds. You are among the few who *ask* for jury duty.

- How could you be boring in bed? Right after dinner, you pass out at the table.

NOVEMBER

25 ANDREW CARNEGIE
JOE DIMAGGIO
RICARDO
  MONTALBAN
JOHN LARROQUETTE

26 CHARLES SCHULZ
ROBERT GOULET
RICH LITTLE
TINA TURNER

27 JIMI HENDRIX
BRUCE LEE
EDDIE RABBIT
CAROLINE KENNEDY

28 RANDY NEWMAN
ED HARRIS
JUDD NELSON
JON STEWART

29 ADAM CLAYTON
  POWELL JR.
CHUCK MANGIONE
GARRY SHANDLING
CATHY MORIARTY

Cancer

June 21 - July 22

WHAT THE STARS SAY...

Cancer, the crab, symbolizes those who are highly protective of themselves and their families. With a love of their homes, they also have a keen business sense. Loyal to friends, they can also be moody and overly sensitive.

THOSE WHO KNOW YOU ADD...

- You are greatly attached to your home. To you, nothing is more exciting than getting a second mortgage.
- Business-minded, you believe that the greatest book ever written is the Yellow Pages.
- You are loyal to your friends. They know they can count on you when you need them.
- You have a tendency toward paranoia. You would really like to join Paranoids Anonymous...but are convinced they won't tell you where they hold their meetings.

| **30** MARK TWAIN
WINSTON
CHURCHILL
DICK CLARK
BEN STILLER | **ALSO BORN**
ON THIS DAY IN
DECEMBER: | **1** WOODY ALLEN
RICHARD PRYOR
BETTE MIDLER
CANDACE
BUSHNELL | **2** MARIA CALLAS
JULIE HARRIS
STONE PHILLIPS
BRITNEY SPEARS | **3** ANDY WILLIAMS
OZZY OSBORNE
DARYL HANNAH
BRENDAN FRASER |

Leo

July 23 – August 22

WHAT THE STARS SAY...

Leo, the lion, is the sign of people who desire to control whatever they encounter and to be the center of attention. They tend to be friendly and enthusiastic. But they can also be pompous and slightly egotistical, and they rarely refuse a drink.

THOSE WHO KNOW YOU ADD...

- Your need for attention is extreme. You even complain when not chosen from a police lineup.

- You can be a friend but also a bitter enemy. This is highly valuable in war...and also useful at PTA meetings.

- Slightly egotistical? When you visit the Statue of Liberty, you are convinced she is carrying the torch for you.

- You really enjoy a strong drink. Last week you dropped a penny on the street, then looked up at the church clock tower...to see how much you weighed.

DECEMBER

4 GENERAL CUSTER
JEFF BRIDGES
MARISA TOMEI
JAY-Z

5 MARTIN VAN BUREN
WALT DISNEY
LITTLE RICHARD
JOSÉ CARRERAS

6 IRA GERSHWIN
DAVE BRUBECK
DON KING
TOM HULCE

7 ELI WALLACH
ELLEN BURSTYN
HARRY CHAPIN
LARRY BIRD

8 JAMES THURBER
SAMMY DAVIS JR.
JIM MORRISON
KIM BASINGER

Virgo
August 23 – September 22

WHAT THE STARS SAY...

Virgo, the virgin, represents people who are energetic with a need to find positive outlets. Hard working, they tend to be meticulous, modest and marriage-minded. They are also analytical and fussy.

THOSE WHO KNOW YOU ADD...

- As a diligent person, you never put off until tomorrow what you can put off indefinitely.

- You are a firm believer in marriage. In fact, you never dated anyone who was not married.

- You recognize that man's greatest labor-saving device is the love of a rich woman.

- Fussy is not the word for it. Whenever you dine out, you send back the menu.

9 KIRK DOUGLAS
REDD FOXX
JUDY DENCH
DONNY OSMOND

10 EMILY DICKINSON
DOROTHY LAMOUR
HAROLD GOULD
SUSAN DEY

11 ALEKSANDR
SOLZHENITSYN
RITA MORENO
BRENDA LEE
TERRI GARR

12 EDWARD G.
ROBINSON
FRANK SINATRA
DIONNE WARWICK
JENNIFER CONNELY

13 BOB BARKER
DICK VAN DYKE
CHRISTOPHER
PLUMMER
JAMIE FOXX

Libra
September 23 – October 22

WHAT THE STARS SAY...

Libra, the scales, is the sign of those who crave balance and harmony in their lives. They tend to be easygoing, polite and diplomatic. Hopelessly romantic, they can also be gullible and self-indulgent.

THOSE WHO KNOW YOU ADD...

• Preferring a leisurely pace, you would never go to Mexico for a vacation...feeling that the pace in Mexico is much too fast.

• You are so polite that, on receiving a letter bomb recently, you wrote back immediately.

• Thoughtful to a fault, whenever you see a woman standing on the bus, you offer her your lap.

• Being romantic, you keep going to City Hall where you were married... to see if your marriage license has expired.

14 NOSTRADAMUS
MOREY AMSTERDAM
LEE REMICK
PATTY DUKE

15 J. PAUL GETTY
ALAN FREED
TIM CONWAY
DON JOHNSON

16 LUDWIG VAN
BEETHOVEN
JANE AUSTIN
NOEL COWARD
LIV ULLMANN

17 NIJINSKI
ARTHUR FIEDLER
WILLIAM SAFIRE
BILL PULLMAN

18 BETTY GRABLE
STEVEN SPIELBERG
BRAD PITT
CHRISTINA
AGUILERA

Scorpio
October 23 – November 21

WHAT THE STARS SAY...

Scorpio, the scorpion, represents people who are powerful and strong-willed, with a respect for authority. Because of their intensity, they display passion and emotions through hard work. They also can become jealous and resentful.

THOSE WHO KNOW YOU ADD...

• You have a great repect for authority. You even salute meter maids.

• You will sometimes become depressed. You were once barred from the circus because the management was afraid you were going to put the clowns in a bad mood.

• Your jealously can be out of control. Last week you looked at your spouse's calendar and demanded to know who April was.

• You are strong-willed and usually have the last word..."I apologize."

19 CICELY TYSON
ROBERT URICH
JENNIFER BEALS
ALYSSA MILANO

20 HARVEY FIRESTONE
URI GELLER
ANITA BAKER
KEIFER
    SUTHERLAND

21 PHIL DONAHUE
JANE FONDA
SAMUEL L.
    JACKSON
RAY ROMANO

22 CHARLES DE GAULLE
MAURICE &
    ROBIN GIBB
DIANE SAWYER
RALPH FIENNES

23 JOSÉ GRECO
HARRY GUARDINO
SUSAN LUCCI
HARRY SHEARER

Sagittarius

November 22 – December 21

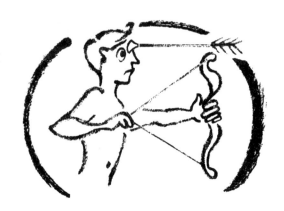

WHAT THE STARS SAY...

Sagittarius, the archer, is the sign of those searching for challenges and adventure. Highly optimistic, they tend to be generous, good-humored and philosophical. But they can also be tactless and irresponsible.

THOSE WHO KNOW YOU ADD...

• As the eternal optimist, you would keep screaming, "I'm not hurt yet" on your way down if you were to fall from a building.

• You enjoy a good challenge. Most memorable was the time you went five whole years without once picking up the check at dinner.

• Seeking adventures, you like to go to orgies...but only to eat the grapes.

• Generous to a fault, you over-tip at pay toilets.

DECEMBER

24 CAB CALLOWAY
HOWARD HUGHES
AVA GARDNER
RICKY MARTIN

25 ISSAC NEWTON
HUMPHREY BOGART
JIMMY BUFFETT
SISSY SPACEK

26 HENRY MILLER
STEVE ALLEN
ALAN KING
DAVID SEDARIS

27 LOUIS PASTEUR
MARLENE DIETRICH
GERARD DÉPARDIEU
COKIE ROBERTS

28 WOODROW WILSON
ROD SERLING
MAGGIE SMITH
DENZEL
WASHINGTON

Capricorn
December 22 – January 19

WHAT THE STARS SAY...

Capricorn, the goat, is a sign of people who are practical and ambitious. Being self-disciplined, they tend to be rigid and stingy. They may also lack self-confidence and tend to be pessimistic, causing them to delay action.

THOSE WHO KNOW YOU ADD...

- Because of your ambition, you have a perfect record at work... never having missed a coffee break in 10 years.

- "Stingy" fits you to a T. You once gave up golf for 15 years... playing again only after you found your ball.

- Your pessimism can be a problem. Whenever opportunity knocks, you complain about the noise.

- You do not worry about tomorrow. You know it will turn out to be terrible.

29 ANDREW JOHNSON
MARY TYLER MOORE
JON VOIGHT
JUDE LAW

30 RUDYARD KIPLING
TRACEY ULLMAN
MATT LAUER
TIGER WOODS

31 HENRI MATISSE
ANTHONY HOPKINS
JOHN DENVER
DONNA SUMMER

THAT'S ALL, FOLKS!

Aquarius
January 20 – February 18

WHAT THE STARS SAY...

Aquarius, the water bearer, represents a quest for independence and achieving the right lifestyle. Humanitarian in nature, people born under this sign are friendly and honest. They can also be distant and even masochistic.

THOSE WHO KNOW YOU ADD...

- You are a humanitarian. After reading that it takes $20 a year to support a child in India, you decided to send your own kids over there.

- You are a champion of the common man. You steal from the rich... so you can sell to the poor.

- Accepting of everyone, you prefer to date homeless people... because it is easier to persuade them to stay over.

- Reluctantly, you gave up masochism. You were enjoying it too much.

Pisces

February 19 – March 19

WHAT THE STARS SAY...

Pisces, the fish, is a sign that reflects the tension between practicality and a yearning for spirituality. People born under this sign tend to be romantic and sensual, often having a sunny outlook. Simultaneously, they can be gullible and deceitful.

THOSE WHO KNOW YOU ADD...

• Some romantic. Your idea of foreplay is announcing, "Honey, I'm home!"

• And sensual? You consider Yoo-hoo to be an aphrodisiac.

• With your sunny outlook, you do not hesitate to go to a fancy restaurant penniless, expecting to pay for the meal with the pearl you will find in your oyster.

• When you find out you are losing your hair, you take pleasure in gaining more forehead.

— And now —

FOR THOSE WHO BELIEVE A PICTURE IS BETTER THAN A LOT OF WORDS...

"It's a birthday card from George. He says I'm his number one. Does that mean there's a number two?"

"Are you interested in an expensive gift, or is it for your wife?"

"See, the pre-nup says, 'Birthday gifts *are* optional after first three years of marriage."

CHAPTER EIGHT

You Made History

JANUARY

1
Ellis Island begins processing immigrants arriving in U.S. (1892).
America's first air-conditioned office building opens in San Antonio, TX (1928).
First woman ordained as Episcopal priest (1977).

2
Mormon leader Brigham Young, who has 25 wives, arrested for bigamy (1872).
Martin Luther King Jr. begins drive to register black voters (1965).
First successful heart transplant performed by Dr. Christian Barnard (1968).

3
Leonardo da Vinci tests his flying machine (1496).
King Tut's gold coffin unearthed by archaeologist Howard Carter (1924).
Alaska admitted as 49th state of the Union (1959).

4
George Washington delivers first State of the Union Address (1790).
Soviet rocket Luna 1 becomes first craft to leave Earth's gravity (1959).
Euro debuts as a single currency in eleven European nations (1999).

5
America's first divorce granted to Anne Clarke of the Massachusetts Bay Colony (1643).
Ford Motor Company establishes $5 minimum wage for 8-hour workday (1914).
President Nixon orders development of space shuttle (1972).

6
First boxing match held in England (1681).
Samuel Morse gives first public demonstration of the telegraph (1838).
Pan Am makes first commercial around-the-world airline flight (1942).

7
Typewriter patented by Englishman Henry Mill (1714).
America's first commercial bank, Bank of North America, opens in Philadelphia (1782).
First U.S. presidential election held (1789).

8
America's first corporation, a New York fishing company, chartered (1675).
World's first soup kitchen opens in London (1800).
First U.S. patent for an electronic computer issued to Dr. Herman Hollerith (1889).

9
Income tax introduced in England (1799).
Civil War begins, as Confederates fire on Fort Sumter in Charleston, SC (1861).
United Nations headquarters officially open in New York (1951).

10
World's first subway opens in London (1863).
John D. Rockefeller incorporates Standard Oil (1870).
World's first jet passenger trip made (1951).

11
World's first recorded lottery drawn in London (1569).
Insulin used for first time to treat diabetes (1922).
America's first discotheque, Whiskey-A-Go-Go, opens in LA (1963).

12
America's first public museum opens, in Charleston, SC (1773).
Dr. Henry Smith takes America's first x-rays (1896).
"All in the Family" premieres on CBS (1971).

13
First ad for a radio set, a $7.50 Telimco, appears in Scientific American (1906).
First-ever radio broadcast, by Lee De Forest, American inventor of the vacuum tube (1910).
First Frisbee produced by Wham-O (1957).

14
Revolutionary War officially ends (1784).
"Today" show premieres on NBC (1952).
Marilyn Monroe marries Joe DiMaggio (1962).

15
Fraunces Tavern, where George Washington bid his troops farewell, opens in NYC (1762).
The Pentagon, covering 34 acres of land, dedicated as world's largest office building (1943).
First Super Bowl played, with Green Bay beating Kansas City 35-10 (1967).

16
Prohibition goes into effect in the U.S. (1919).
League of Nations assembles for first time, in Paris (1920).
Operation Desert Storm begins, with U.S. driving Iraqi army out of Kuwait (1991).

17
Capt. James Cook becomes first person to cross Antarctic Circle (1773).
Great Brinks Robbery: thieves snatch $2 million from armored car in Boston (1950).
Nautilus begins first nuclear-powered submarine voyage (1955).

18
America's first UFO sighting, by Pilgrims in Boston (1644).
Capt. James Cook discovers Hawaii (1778).
First demonstration of x-ray machine in the U.S. (1896).

19
Charles Wilkes discovers Antarctica and claims it for U.S. (1840).
68% of all Americans watch CBS as Lucy Ricardo gives birth on "I Love Lucy" (1953).
U.S. and Iran sign agreement to release 52 American hostages (1981).

20
Roller coaster patented by La Marcus Thompson of Coney Island, NY (1885).
World's first organized basketball game played in Massachusetts (1892).
Franklin Roosevelt sworn in for unprecedented 4th term as president (1945).

JANUARY

21
America's first novel, "The Power of Sympathy," published anonymously in Boston (1789).
Gold hits all-time record high of $850 an ounce (1980).
Census Bureau estimates U.S. Hispanic population passes African-American population (2003).

22
Uranium atom split for first time, at New York's Columbia University (1939).
Supreme Court legalizes abortion in Roe v. Wade (1973).
Apple Macintosh computer introduced (1984).

23
First English Parliament convenes (1265).
Robert E. Lee named commander-in-chief of Confederate Armies (1865)
President Nixon announces accord to end Vietnam War (1973).

24
Discovery of gold in California sets off gold rush (1848).
World's first canned beer introduced in Richmond, VA (1935).
U.S. Department of Homeland Security begins operations (2003).

25
Alexander Graham Bell places first transcontinental telephone call (1915).
First Winter Olympic games open in Chamonix, France (1924).
First Emmy Awards presented by Academy of Television Arts and Sciences (1949).

26
World's largest diamond, the 3,106-carat Cullinan, found in South Africa (1905).
President Truman signs order ending segregation in U.S. armed forces (1948).
Americans with Disabilities Act goes into effect (1992).

27
World's first TV broadcast demonstrated by Scotsman John Logie Baird (1926).
America's involvement in Vietnam War ends (1973).
U.S. stages first air attack on Germany, over Wilhelmshafen, during World War II (1943).

28
World's first telephone switchboard installed in New Haven, CT (1878).
John Brown raids federal arsenal at Harper's Ferry, WV, hoping to lead slave rebellion (1858).
Norway elects 101-year-old prime minister, Christopher Hornsrud (1928).

29
World's first gasoline-powered car patented by Karl Benz in Germany (1886).
Liliuokalani proclaimed Queen of Hawaii, islands' last monarch (1891).
Walt Disney starts his first job as an artist, with Kansas City Slide Co. (1920).

30
U.S. government issues first Social Security check, to secretary who lives to be 100 (1940).
America's first space satellite, Explorer I, goes into orbit (1958).
Beatles perform last gig together, in London (1969).

FEBRUARY

1
America's first auto-insurance policy issued by Travelers Insurance (1898).
First Miss America, Edith Hyde, a mother of two, crowned in New York City (1919).
Presidents George Bush and Boris Yeltsin sign agreement ending Cold War (1992).

2
New Amsterdam (later New York) becomes a city (1653).
World War II's Battle of Stalingrad ends with surrender of German army (1943).
Allied troops set foot on Japanese territory for first time during World War II (1944).

3
America's first paper money issued by Massachusetts colony (1690).
Federal income tax established with ratification of 16th Amendment (1913).
Soviet spacecraft Luna 9 makes world's first soft (non-crash) moon landing (1966).

4
Electoral College chooses George Washington as president (1789).
Free African-Americans settle Liberia, West Africa (1822).
First portable electric typewriter sold (1957).

5
First motion picture shown to a theater audience, in Philadelphia (1870).
First issue of Reader's Digest published (1922).
U.S. airlines begin mandatory inspection of passengers and luggage (1972).

6
Spanish-American War ends (1899).
America's first old-age home opens in Arizona (1911).
Frank Sinatra makes radio debut on "Your Hit Parade" (1943).

7
Ballet introduced to U.S., at New York's Bowery Theatre (1827).
Beatles arrive at New York's Kennedy Airport on first U.S. visit (1964).
European Union established with signing of Maastricht Treaty (1992).

8
Mary Queen of Scots beheaded for plot to murder Queen Elizabeth I (1587).
Confederate States of America organized in Montgomery, AL, during Civil War (1861).
Boy Scouts of America incorporated, in Chicago (1910).

9
Daylight-saving time goes into effect in U.S. (1942).
Normandie, world's most elegant ocean liner, burns and sinks in New York Harbor (1942).
Satchel Paige becomes first Negro League player voted into Baseball Hall of Fame (1971).

10
French and Indian War ends (1763).
Fire extinguisher patented (1863).
World War II peace treaties signed (1947).

FEBRUARY

11
America's first hospital, Pennsylvania Hospital, opens in Philadelphia (1752).
Steamboat patented by Robert Fulton (1809).
Fourteen-year-old peasant girl in France claims to see Virgin Mary (1858).

12
First artificial ice rink in North America, Madison Square Garden in New York, opens (1879).
National Association for the Advancement of Colored People founded (1909).
President Clinton acquitted on impeachment charges (1999).

13
Galileo brought before Italian Inquisition for believing Earth revolves around sun (1633).
Abraham Lincoln declared president (1861).
Jesse James robs his first bank, stealing $60,000 (1866).

14
First photograph of U.S. President (James Polk) taken by Matthew Brady (1849).
IBM Corp. founded (1924).
First "micro on a chip" patented by Texas Instruments (1978).

15
Mysterious explosion sinks the USS Maine in Cuba's Havana Harbor (1898).
World's first teddy bear, named after Teddy Roosevelt, introduced (1903).
St. Valentine's Day massacre carried out in Chicago (1929).

16
First commercial helicopter tested, in Bridgeport, CT (1946).
Fidel Castro names himself prime minister of Cuba, overthrowing Fulgencio Batista (1959).
Largest jewel heist, $100 million in precious stones from Antwerp Diamond Center (2003).

17
War of 1812 ends as U.S. and Britain sign Treaty of Ghent. (1815).
First ship passes through Suez Canal (1867).
First issue of Newsweek magazine published (1933).

18
America's first filibuster begins, tying up Senate for 23 days (1841).
Pluto, farthest planet from the sun, discovered (1930).
First Iron Man Triathlon, requiring swimming, biking and running, held in Hawaii (1978).

19
Vice President Aaron Burr arrested in Alabama for treason, and later found innocent (1807).
Thomas Edison patents the phonograph (1878).
First test flight of Boeing 747 jumbo jet (1969).

20
U.S. Postal Department created (1792).
Metropolitan Museum of Art opens in New York City (1872).
John Glenn orbits Earth three times (1962).

FEBRUARY

21
America's first telephone books distributed in New Haven, CT (1878).
Malcolm X assassinated in Harlem, NY (1965).
Richard Nixon becomes first U.S. president to visit China (1972).

22
First organized baseball game played, in San Francisco (1860).
First Woolworth's "five and ten cent" store opens in Utica, NY (1879).
Transcontinental airmail service begins in the U.S. (1923).

23
Johannes Gutenberg begins work on his Bible, the world's first printed book (1452).
U.S. Marines raise American flag on Iwo Jima during World War II (1945).
First cloned mammal, a lamb named Dolly, announced by scientists in Scotland (1997).

24
House of Representatives votes to impeach President Andrew Johnson (1868).
First rocket to reach outer space launched in New Mexico (1949).
World's first baby conceived through in vitro fertilization born in London (1978).

25
America's first black congressman, Hiram Revels, sworn in (1870).
"Your Show of Shows" with Sid Caesar premieres on NBC (1950).
Cassius Clay, 22, wins heavyweight boxing title by defeating Sonny Liston (1964).

26
First New York City subway line opens (1870).
Congress establishes Grand Canyon National Park in Colorado (1919).
World's first red-and-green traffic lights installed, in Manhattan (1930).

27
Saccharin discovered (1879).
First issue of People magazine published (1974).
Tiger Woods, 16, becomes youngest PGA golfer in 35 years (1992).

28
First vaudeville theater opens in Boston (1883).
125 million watch final episode of "MASH," highest-rated show in U.S. history (1983).
U.S. and Allied forces grant Iraq a ceasefire in Gulf War (1991).

29
Christopher Columbus uses lunar eclipse to frighten hostile Jamaican Indians (1504).
First arrest warrants issued for women in Salem, MA, accused of witchcraft (1692).
First Chinese immigrants arrive in San Francisco (1848).

MARCH

1
U.S. federal income tax takes effect (1913).
Charles Lindbergh's son kidnapped in New Jersey (1932).
Peace Corps established by President Kennedy (1961).

2
Americans begin shelling British troops in Boston during Revolutionary War (1776).
First issue of Time magazine published (1923).
Texas separates from Mexico and proclaims independence (1836).

3
U.S. Steel Corp. founded (1900).
"The Star-Spangled Banner" becomes America's national anthem (1931).
Elvis Presley makes first TV appearance (1955).

4
First session of Congress held in New York City (1789).
"Happy Birthday to You" published by Claydon Sunny (1924).
U.S. nuclear submarine Nautilus becomes first vessel to pass under North Pole's icecap (1958).

5
British troops fire on crowd of civilians in the Boston Massacre (1770).
Colt manufactures its first pistol, the .34-caliber "Texas" (1836).
Winston Churchill coins the term "Iron Curtain" (1946).

6
Battle of the Alamo ends after 13-day siege (1836).
Aspirin patented by Felix Hoffmann (1899).
Clarence Birdseye develops method for quick-freezing food (1930).

7
Henry VIII declares himself head of England's church after pope denies divorce request (1530).
Dr. John Kellog invents corn flakes in Battle Creek, MI (1897).
Mike Tyson, 20, wins youngest heavyweight boxing title, beating James Smith in Las Vegas (1987).

8
First helicopter licensed for commercial use (1946).
Supreme Court rules religious instruction in public schools unconstitutional (1948).
Goodyear Blimp makes maiden voyage (1972).

9
Napoleon Bonaparte marries Josephine de Beauharnais (1796).
Artificial teeth patented by Charles Graham of New York (1822).
French Foreign Legion formed (1831).

10
Alexander Graham Bell makes first phone call, to his assistant, Mr. Watson (1876).
Salvation Army of England arrives in America to set up welfare programs (1880).
Nasdaq peaks at 5048.62, signaling beginning of the end of dot-com boom (2000).

MARCH

11
Romeo and Juliet are married, according to Shakespeare (1302).
"The Godfather" premieres (1972).
An American B-47 accidentally drops nuclear bomb on S. Carolina; it does not go off (1953).

12
Girl Scouts of America founded (1912).
Mahatma Gandhi embarks on his "salt march" to protest British salt tax (1930).
U.S. lowers voting age from 21 to 18 (1970).

13
U.S. Senate begins impeachment trial of President Andrew Johnson (1868).
A Tennessee law prohibits teaching of evolution (1925).
Sister Nirmala succeeds Mother Teresa as leader of the Missionaries of Charity (1997).

14
Eli Whitney patents cotton gin (1794).
U.S. currency backed by gold bullion, with ratification of Gold Standard Act (1900).
FBI debuts "10 Most Wanted Fugitives" list (1950).

15
Emperor Julius Caesar assassinated in Roman Senate (44 BC).
Charles Rolls and Henry Royce establish Rolls-Royce in London (1906).
America's first blood bank established at Chicago's Cook County Hospital (1937).

16
U.S. Military Academy at West Point established (1802).
National Gallery of Art opens in Washington, DC (1941).
U.S. defeats Japan at Iwo Jima during WWII (1945).

17
Noah and his menagerie board the Ark, according to the Bible.
U.S. issues first paper money, in denominations of $5, $10 and $20 (1862).
First practical submarine submerges in New York Harbor (1898).

18
Schick introduces first electric shaver (1931).
North Atlantic Treaty Organization, a defensive alliance against communist East, ratified (1949).
World's first plastic contact lenses fitted in Philadelphia (1952).

19
First bank robbery in America, with $245,000 taken from City Bank of New York (1831).
Nevada legalizes gambling (1931).
U.S.-led forces invade Iraq (Operation Iraqi Freedom) to oust Saddam Hussein (2003).

20
Republican Party founded (1854).
Gen. MacArthur vows, "I shall return," as he leaves Philippines at end of World War II (1942).
John Lennon marries Yoko Ono on Rock of Gibraltar (1969).

MARCH

21
D.J. Alan Freed presents world's first rock 'n' roll concert in Cleveland (1952).
Alcatraz Federal Penitentiary in San Francisco Bay closed (1963).
Martin Luther King Jr. begins civil rights from Selma to Montgomery, AL (1965).

22
Carbonated water invented (1733).
British Parliament passes Stamp Act, first tax levied on American colonies (1765).
World's first airline, St. Petersburg Tampa Airboat, begins service (1914).

23
American patriot Patrick Henry proclaims, "Give me liberty or give me death" (1775).
Wright brothers patent their airplane (1903).
First telephone installed in White House (1929).

24
First televised religious services, in New York City (1930).
Elvis Presley joins U.S. Army (1958).
Astronaut Shannon Lucid enters Russia's Mir, becoming first U.S. woman to live in space. (1996).

25
Venice founded (421).
First modern Olympic games in Athens, where American James Connolly wins first event (1896).
RCA introduces first color-TV set, priced at $1,000 (1954).

26
George Washington chops down father's cherry tree (1746).
Dr. Jonas Salk announces discovery of polio vaccine (1953).
"Funny Girl" with Barbra Streisand opens on Broadway (1964).

27
First successful blood transfusion performed in Brussels (1914).
Nikita Khrushchev becomes Soviet premier (1958).
CBS Labs introduces stereophonic records (1958).

28
Washing machine patented (1797).
America's first ambulance goes into service in Maine (1866).
Spanish Civil War ends (1939).

29
King Henry VIII marries sixth and final wife, Katherine Parr (1543).
Ludwig von Beethoven, 24, debuts as a pianist, in Vienna (1795).
Dow closes above 10,000 for first time (1999).

30
Crawford Long becomes first doctor to use anesthesia during an operation (1842).
U.S. buys Alaska from Russia for $7.2 million, or 2¢ an acre (1867).
President Reagan shot by John Hinckley Jr. (1981).

31
Eiffel Tower opens in Paris (1889).
Daylight savings time takes effect in U.S. (1918).
America's first dance marathon held in New York, with winner lasting 27 hours (1923).

APRIL

1
U.S. launches invasion of Okinawa during World War II (1945).
First U.S. weather satellite launched (1960).
U.S. formally transfers Canal Zone to Panamá (1982).

2
Ponce de León discovers Florida (1513).
Titanic sets sail from Ireland on her maiden voyage (1912).
Velcro introduced (1978).

3
Harvard College confers first honorary degree, to George Washington (1776).
Pony Express mail service begins (1860).
First issue of TV Guide published (1953).

4
City of Los Angeles incorporated (1850).
Vitamin C first isolated, at University of Pittsburgh (1932).
Martin Luther King Jr. assassinated in Memphis (1968).

5
Last surviving Revolutionary War soldier dies at age 109 (1869).
Firestone begins manufacturing inflatable tires (1923).
World Trade Center Towers, then world's tallest buildings, opens (1974).

6
Robert Perry and Matthew Henson become first people to reach North Pole (1909).
America enters World War I (1917).
First Tony Awards presented at New York's Waldorf-Astoria Hotel (1947).

7
First commercial computer, IBM 701 Electronic Data Processing Machine, introduced (1953).
Oklahoma ends prohibition after 51 years (1959).
Internet created, at University of California (1969).

8
First aerosol dispenser patented (1862).
First legal off-track betting system begins in New York (1971).
Hank Aaron hits 715th home run, breaking Babe Ruth's all-time record (1974).

9
Capt. James Cook discovers Australia (1770).
America's first public library opens in New Hampshire (1833).
Robert E. Lee surrenders to Ulysses S. Grant at Appomattox (1865).

10
Capt. Robert Gray becomes first American to circumnavigate globe (1790).
Walter Hunt invents the safety pin, selling his patent for $100 (1849).
American Society for Prevention of Cruelty to Animals founded (1866).

APRIL

11
Vatican confirms sainthood on Joan of Arc (1909).
Jackie Robinson becomes first black player in major-league baseball (1947).
First nonstop around-the-world sailboat voyage completed (1986).

12
Confederate troops attack Fort Sumter, setting off Civil War (1861).
First space shuttle, Columbia, launched from Cape Canaveral (1981).
Harvard University patents first genetically engineered animal, a mouse (1988).

13
JC Penney opens first store, in Wyoming (1902).
Apollo 13 warns, "Houston, we've got a problem!" as oxygen tank explodes in space (1970).
Tiger Woods becomes youngest winner of Master's Golf Tourney; sets 72-hole record (1997).

14
President Lincoln assassinated in Washington, DC (1865).
Thomas Edison's Kinetoscope first appears in a New York City arcade (1894).
Marie and Pierre Curie discover radium (1902).

15
First telephone installed in Boston (1877).
Titanic sinks off coast of Newfoundland (1912).
First McDonald's restaurant opens in Des Planes, IL (1955).

16
Vladimir Lenin returns from exile to lead Russian Revolution (1917).
Book-of-the-Month Club sends out first selections (1926).
Two giant pandas arrive in U.S. as gift from China (1972).

17
Martin Luther excommunicated from Roman Catholic Church (1521).
Igor Sikorsky accomplishes first successful helicopter lift-off (1941).
Apollo 13 returns safely to Earth, after being stranded in space (1970).

18
Paul Revere rides through Boston warning, "The British are coming!" (1775).
Yankee Stadium opens in the Bronx (1923).
U.S. General James Doolittle bombs Tokyo during World War II (1942).

19
Revolutionary War begins with battles at Lexington and Concord (1775).
America's first marathon, the Boston Marathon, won by John McDermott (1897).
Oklahoma City Federal Building bombed (1995).

20
Harriet Tubman begins her Underground Railroad (1853).
Supreme Court upholds use of busing for racial desegregation (1971).
Chicago Bulls end season with record 72 wins in one season (1996).

APRIL

21
Rome founded (753 BC).
Noah Webster publishes first American dictionary (1828).
Russia's Red Army captures Berlin during World War II (1945).

22
Henry VIII becomes King of England (1509).
World's Fair opens in New York City (1964).
First Earth Day observed (1970).

23
William Shakespeare dies and is buried in Stratford (1616).
Elvis Presley makes first Las Vegas appearance (1956).
Coca-Cola changes its 99-year-old secret formula (1985).

24
Library of Congress established (1800).
Eastman Kodak founded (1888).
Spain declares war on U.S. (1898).

25
Guillotine used for first time, executing a French highwayman (1792).
Scientists identify DNA (1953).
Hubble Space Telescope put into orbit by Discovery space shuttle (1990).

26
Smallpox vaccination first administrated (1721).
Madame Tussaud's first wax museum opens in London (1928).
New York's famed disco Studio 54 opens (1977).

27
Computer mouse introduced by Xerox (1973).
First atomic-powered electric-drive submarine launched (1960).
Beijing students take over Tiananmen Square in China (1989).

28
Air conditioner patented by Willis Carrier (1914).
Yellow fever vaccine for humans announced (1932).
Soviet nuclear power plant in Chernobyl catches fire (1986).

29
Zipper patented (1913).
Construction of Lindbergh's Spirit of St. Louis completed (1927).
U.S. forces pull out of Vietnam (1975).

30
George Washington inaugurated as America's first president (1789).
First practical typewriter developed, in Italy (1808).
Ice cream cone debuts (1904).

MAY

1
New York's Empire State Building opens (1931).
First Batman comic book published (1939).
Orson Welles' "Citizen Kane" opens in New York (1941).

2
First issue of Good Housekeeping published (1885).
General Motors acquires Chevrolet Motor Company (1918).
First commercial jet plane, BOAC Comet, goes into service (1952).

3
Washington, DC, incorporated as a city (1802).
National Public Radio debuts (1971).
First airplane, a modified U.S. Air Force C-47, lands on North Pole (1952).

4
Governor Peter Minuit buys Manhattan from Native Americans for $24 (1626).
Academy of Motion Picture Arts & Sciences founded (1927).
Four students at Ohio's Kent State University shot by National Guard (1970).

5
American Medical Association organized in Philadelphia (1847).
Carnegie Hall opens in New York, with Tchaikovsky as guest conductor (1891).
Astronaut Alan Shepard becomes first American in space (1961).

6
German zepplin Hindenberg explodes while docking in New Jersey (1937).
Joseph Stalin becomes premier of Russia (1941).
Channel Tunnel linking England and France opens (1994).

7
Betsy Ross completes sewing of first stars-and-stripes American flag (1776).
British ocean liner Lusitania sunk by German submarine (1915).
Winston Churchill becomes British Prime Minister (1940).

8
Coca-Cola sold for first time, at a soda fountain in an Atlanta pharmacy (1886).
Germany surrenders to Allied Forces (V-E Day), ending WWII in Europe (1945).
Hernando de Soto discovers Mississippi River (1541).

9
Columbus leaves Spain on fouth and final trip to New World (1502).
America's first gaslit theatre, the Chatham, opens in New York (1825).
Beatles sign their first recording contract (1962).

10
Ben Franklin first tests the lightning rod (1752).
First U.S. naval ship, the United States, launched (1797).
America's first trans-continental railroad completed (1869).

MAY

11
America's first fire-insurance policy issued (1752).
Waltz introduced into English ballrooms (1812).
First contraceptive pill goes on the market in U.S. (1960).

12
Wireless radio broadcasting patented (1908).
State of Israel established (1948).
Last episode of "Cheers" broadcast on NBC (1993).

13
Diner's Club issues first-ever credit card (1950).
Pope John Paul II shot in St. Peter's Square (1981).
Students begin hunger strike in Tiananmen Square, China (1989).

14
Jamestown, VA, becomes first permanent settlement in New World (1607).
First Olympic games in U.S. open in St. Louis (1904).
Skylab, world's first space station, launched (1973).

15
City of Las Vegas founded (1905).
First U.S. airmail service begins (1918).
Nylon hose go on sale throughout U.S. (1940).

16
First steamboat introduced on Mississippi River (1817).
First Academy Awards presented in Hollywood (1929).
U.S. Surgeon General reports nicotine is addictive (1988).

17
New York Stock Exchange established (1792).
First Kentucky Derby run (1875).
Supreme Court outlaws segregation (1954).

18
Rhode Island becomes first colony to outlaw slavery (1652).
Napoleon Bonaparte proclaimed Emperor of France (1804).
Mt. St. Helens erupts in Washington State (1980).

19
Ringling Bros. circus premieres (1884).
First person convicted of a crime through use of fingerprints (1911).
Lawrence of Arabia dies in motorcycle accident (1935).

20
Levi Strauss begins marketing blue jeans (1874).
First regular transatlantic airmail begins (1939).
Igor Sikorsky unveils his invention, the helicopter (1940).

MAY

21
American Red Cross founded by Clara Barton (1881).
Charles Lindbergh completes world's first solo transatlantic flight (1927).
Amelia Earhart becomes first woman to fly solo across Atlantic (1932).

22
Mary Kies of Connecticut becomes first American woman issued a patent (1809).
Associated Press founded in New York as non-profit news cooperative (1900).
Johnny Carson hosts "The Tonight Show" for last time (1992).

23
Ben Franklin announces his invention of bifocals (1785).
Bonnie and Clyde shot to death by Texas Rangers in Louisiana (1934).
Nazi war criminal Adolf Eichmann captured in Argentina (1960).

24
Samuel Morse sends first Morse Code message (1844).
Brooklyn Bridge opens as then-world's longest suspension bridge (1883).
World's first auto-repair shop opens in Boston (1899).

25
Founding Fathers begin writing Constitution in Philadelphia (1787).
Movietone News, first regular newsreel, debuts, showing Lindbergh's Paris landing (1927).
"Star Wars" premieres (1977).

26
President Andrew Johnson's impeachment trial ends in "not guilty" verdict (by one vote) (1868).
U.S. and Soviet Union sign SALT Accord, limiting offensive nuclear missiles (1972).
Resorts International, first legal casino in eastern U.S., opens in Atlantic City (1978).

27
Bubonic Plague breaks out in San Francisco (1907).
Federal Securities Act, requiring federal registration of stocks, signed into law (1933).
San Francisco's Golden Gate Bridge opens (1937).

28
First indoor swimming pool opens in London (1742).
U.S. Attorney General rules it is legal for women to wear trousers (1923).
Amnesty International founded (1961).

29
Abe Lincoln says, "You can't fool all of the people all of the time" (1849).
"White Christmas" recorded by Bing Crosby (1942).
Edmund Hillary becomes first to reach top of Mt. Everest (1953).

30
Joan of Arc burned at the stake for heresy (1431).
America's first daily paper, Pennsylvania Evening Post, published (1783).
Lincoln Memorial dedicated in Washington, DC (1922).

31
Protesting taxes, Lady Godiva rides naked through Coventry, England (1678).
First jazz record, "Darktown Stutters' Ball," released (1917).
"Seinfeld" premieres on NBC (1990).

JUNE

1
First recorded earthquake in U.S. strikes Plymouth, MA (1638).
First Superman comic book published (1938).
CNN goes on air for first time (1980).

2
P.T. Barnum's circus begins first U.S. tour (1835).
Elizabeth II crowned Queen of England (1953).
New Jersey legalizes casino gambling in Atlantic City (1977).

3
Hernando De Soto claims Florida for Spain (1539).
John Adams moves to Washington, DC, becoming first president to live in nation's capital (1800).
King Edward VIII abdicates British throne to marry American divorceé Wallis Simpson (1937).

4
Total solar eclipse recorded for first time ever, in China (780 BC).
Henry Ford test-drives his first automobile, the Quadricycle (1896).
First-ever Pulitzer Prize awarded, for a biography of Julia Ward Howe (1917).

5
Robert F. Kennedy assassinated in L.A. (1968).
Apple II, world's first personal computer, goes on sale (1977).
U.S. Centers for Disease Control reports existence of AIDS (1981).

6
America's first drive-in theater opens in Camden, NJ (1933).
Allied troops invade beaches of Normandy (D-Day) (1944).
"The Ed Sullivan Show" ends CBS run (1971).

7
Vatican City becomes sovereign state (1929).
First TV quiz show, "The $64,000 Question," premieres on CBS (1955).
Elvis's Graceland mansion opens to public (1982).

8
Islam founded in Mecca (570).
Ice cream manufactured for first time in New York City (1786).
First vacuum cleaner patented (1869).

9
Thomas Morton becomes first person deported from American colonies, due to debauchery (1628).
World's first root beer sold in Philadelphia (1869).
China leases Hong Kong to Great Britain for 99 years (1898).

10
Dutch settlers colonize Manhattan (1610).
Alcoholics Anonymous founded in Ohio (1935).
Janis Joplin gives her first concert, in San Francisco (1966).

JUNE

11 Greek army captures Troy (1184 BC).
Comstock Silver Lode discovered near Virginia City, NV (1859).
Gov. George Wallace tries to prevent black students from enrolling at U. of Alabama (1963).

12 Napoleon invades Russia (1812).
Baseball Hall of Fame opens in Cooperstown, NY (1939).
Ronald Reagan proclaims, "Mr. Gorbachev, tear down this wall!" in Berlin (1987).

13 Oldest known treaty, between England and Portugal, signed (1373).
Supreme Court rules police must inform suspects of rights before questioning (1966).
Pioneer 10 becomes first man-made object to leave solar system (1983).

14 U.S. Army founded (1775).
John Adams establishes stars-and-stripes design as official American flag (1777).
Warren Harding becomes first U.S. president to appear on radio (1922).

15 Magna Carta, granting rights to Englishmen, signed by King John (1215).
Ben Franklin discovers electricity (1752).
George Washington appointed commander-in-chief of American Army (1775).

16 Abraham Lincoln says, "A house divided against itself cannot stand" (1858).
Pepsi-Cola Beverage Co. officially registers its name (1903).
First helicopter flight accomplished by Henry Berliner, in Maryland (1922).

17 Battle of Bunker Hill fought (1775)
Charles Goodyear obtains first rubber patent (1837).
Statue of Liberty arrives in New York from France (1885).

18 War of 1812 begins as America declares war on Britain (1812).
Napoleon defeated in Battle of Waterloo (1815).
Susan B. Anthony fined $100 for attempting to vote (1873).

19 First organized baseball game played, in New Jersey (1846).
U.S. government establishes 8-hour workday (1912).
"Cats" becomes longest-running show on Broadway, with 6138 performances (1997).

20 Queen Victoria ascends British throne at 18 years old (1837).
U.S. and Soviet Union set up emergency hotline during Cold War (1963).
First oil moves through Alaska Pipeline (1977).

JUNE

21
F.W. Woolworth opens his first store (1879).
First Ferris Wheel premieres, at Chicago's Columbian Exposition (1893).
An early computer, built at UK's University of Manchester, runs world's first program (1948).

22
Pope forces Galileo to recant theory that Earth orbits the sun (1633).
Doughnut invented (1847).
America's first water-ski tournament held at New York's Jones Beach (1939).

23
U.S. Secret Service created (1860).
Harvard Medical School graduates first women (1949).
Lorena Bobbitt amputates husband's manhood (1993).

24
First major exhibition of Pablo Picasso's artwork opens in Paris (1901).
TV cameras used for first time at a U.S. presidential-election convention (1940).
Home video recorder demonstrated for first time in London's BBC Studios (1963).

25
Crazy Horse defeats Custer at Battle of Little Bighorn (1876).
Korean War begins (1950).
Supreme Court rules that public-school prayer violates separation of church and state (1962).

26
First French Grand Prix held in Le Mans (1906).
United Nations Charter signed by 50 nations (1945).
Andrea Doria sinks off coast of Cape Cod, MA (1956).

27
First women's magazine, The Ladies' Mercury, published in London (1693).
FBI captures 8 Nazi saboteurs in submarine off New York's Long Island (1942).
World's first nuclear power plant, in Russia, begins generating electricity (1954).

28
World's first dog show held in England (1859).
World War I begins with assassination of Archduke Ferdinand of Austria (1914).
World War I ends with signing of Treaty of Versailles (1919).

29
Shakespeare's Globe Theater burns down (1613).
Billy Haley's "Rock Around the Clock," first rock 'n' roll single, hits No. 1 (1955).
Supreme Court rules capital punishment unconstitutional (1972)

30
Margaret Mitchell's "Gone with the Wind" published (1936).
995.2-carat Excelsior diamond discovered in Africa (1893).
President Truman orders U.S. troops into Korea (1950).

JULY

1
America's first postage stamps go on sale (1847).
Congress outlaws polygamy (1862).
America's first zoo, the Philadelphia Zoological Society, opens (1874).

2
New York City's first elevated railroad opens (1867).
President Garfield shot by disappointed office-seeker Charles Guiteau (1881).
President Johnson signs Civil Rights Act into law (1964).

3
America's first savings bank opens in New York (1819).
Lou Gehrig bids Yankee Stadium farewell with the immortal words, "I am the luckiest man alive" (1939).
Renovated Statue of Liberty dedicated by President Reagan (1986).

4
America's Declaration of Independence approved (1776).
"America" sung publicly for first time (1832).
France presents Statue of Liberty to U.S., in Paris (1884).

5
Isaac Newton's "Principia" published by England's Royal Society (1687).
World's first travel agency opened by Thomas Cook (1841).
Bikini introduced at Paris fashion show (1946).

6
Congress resolves that basic unit of U.S. currency will be called the "dollar" (1785).
First talking motion picture, "The Lights of New York," premieres in New York (1928).
First Beatles' film, "Hard Day's Night," premiers in London (1964).

7
America's first military draft goes into effect (1863).
Doc Holliday and Wyatt Earp fight Clanton gang at O.K. Corral in Tombstone, AZ (1881).
Mother Frances Xavier Cabrini canonized as first American saint (1946).

8
State Department issues America's first passport (1796).
Florenz Ziegfeld stages first "Ziegfeld Follies" (1907).
First issue of The Wall Street Journal published (1889).

9
First passenger helicopter service begins operations, in New York (1953).
First natural-gas well in U.S. discovered (1815).
First Wimbledon tennis championship played (1877).

10
Howard Hughes begins record-setting, around-the-world flight (1938).
650,000 American steel workers go on strike (1956).
Telstar communications satellite launched, revolutionizing global TV and telephone transmission (1962).

JULY

11
Vice President Aaron Burr kills Treasury Secretary Alexander Hamilton in duel (1804).
Phrase "In God We Trust" added to all U.S. currency (1955).
Earth's population crosses 5 billion mark, according to United Nations (1987).

12
Babe Ruth makes his major-league baseball debut (1914).
Minimum wage of 30 cents an hour established in U.S. (1933).
Rolling Stones give first public performance, in London (1962).

13
Women compete in modern Olympic games for first time (1908).
First World Cup soccer match held in Uruguay (1930).
"Live Aid" concert for African famine relief held, drawing 1.5 billion TV viewers (1985).

14
French Revolution begins with storming of Bastille (1789).
"Draft Riot" in New York City, protesting Civil War draft, suppressed by federal troops (1863).
Dr. Benjamin Spock's landmark "Baby and Child Care" published (1946).

15
First Crusade: Christian soldiers take Jerusalem (1099).
Native-American athlete Jim Thorpe wins decathlon at Olympic games in Stockholm (1912).
First airport hotel opens, in Oakland (1929).

16
Kissing banned in England (1439).
Father Junipero Serra founds California's first mission (1769).
First atomic bomb detonated, in Alamagordo, NM (1945).

17
Harvard College Observatory takes first photograph of a star (1850).
World's first commercial air-conditioning system installed in New York (1901).
Disneyland opens in Anaheim, CA (1955).

18
Rome burns while Emperor Nero fiddles (64).
Spanish Civil War begins (1936).
Intel, inventor of microchip, incorporated (1968).

19
America's first women's-rights convention held in Seneca Falls, NY (1848).
World's first in-flight movie shown by TWA (1961).
First air-conditioned New York City subway car (1967).

20
Sioux leader Sitting Bull surrenders to federal troops at Little Big Horn "massacre" (1881).
Apollo 11's Neil Armstrong becomes first human to walk on moon (1969).
America's Viking 1 lander becomes first spacecraft to land on Mars (1976).

JULY

21
Harvard bestows America's first honorary degree on John Winthrop (1733).
Confederates win Battle of Bull Run, first major Civil War battle (1861).
Jesse James pulls off his first train robbery (1873).

22
"America the Beautiful" written by Katharine Lee Bates (1893).
Aviator Wiley Post completes world's first solo around-the-world flight (1933).
John Dillinger gunned down by FBI agents at Chicago's Biograph Theatre (1934).

23
America's first swimming school opens in Boston (1827).
First Ford Model A delivered to its owner (1903).
President Lyndon Johnson declares "War on Poverty" (1964).

24
America's first opinion poll appears in The Harrisburg Pennsylvanian (1824).
Brigham Young and Mormon followers arrive in Salt Lake City (1847).
Tennessee becomes first state re-admitted to Union following Civil War (1866).

25
First steam locomotive introduced (1814).
Puerto Rico becomes self-governing U.S. commonwealth (1952).
World's first test-tube baby born in England (1978).

26
Ben Franklin becomes America's first Postmaster General (1775).
First sugar-cane plantation started in Hawaii (1835).
Federal Bureau of Investigation established (1908).

27
Sir Walter Raleigh brings first tobacco to England from Virginia (1586).
Korean War ends (1953).
House Judiciary Committee votes to impeach President Nixon (1974).

28
Singing telegram introduced, with Rudy Vallee as first recipient (1933).
B-25 bomber crashes into New York's Empire State Building (1945).
World's first hamburger served at Louie's Lunch in New Haven, CT (1895).

29
America's first motorcycle race held at New York's Manhattan Beach (1899).
Transcontinental telephone service inaugurated (1915).
World's first TV program, an RCA variety show, broadcast from New York (1936).

30
Virginia creates House of Burgesses, first elective governing body in American colonies (1619).
"In God We Trust" adopted as America's official motto (1956).
President Johnson signs bill creating Medicare (1965).

31
First U.S. patent issued, for a potash-making process (1790).
Ralph Samuelson, 18, tries out world's first water skis on Lake Pepin, MN (1922).
Apollo 15 astronauts travel on moon in lunar rover (1971).

AUGUST

1
First cablecar begins operation in San Francisco (1873).
First Atlantic crossing in a rowboat (1894).
Woodward and Bernstein publish first report exposing Watergate scandal (1972).

2
New York's famed Fifth Avenue opens for traffic (1824).
America's Declaration of Independence signed (1776).
Iraq invades Kuwait (1990).

3
Congress passes first law restricting immigration (1882).
First aerial cropdusting, in Ohio (1921).
Los Del Rio's "Macarena" hits No. 1, starting new dance craze (1996).

4
Dom Perignon invents champagne (1693).
Saturday Evening Post published for first time (1821).
U.S. Coast Guard founded as Revenue Cutter Service (1790).

5
America's first traffic light installed in Cleveland (1914).
America drops atom bomb on Hiroshima (1945).
Mark McGwire hits home run No. 500 on 5,487th at-bat, beating Babe Ruth's record (1999).

6
Gertrude Ederle, 19, becomes first woman to swim English Channel (1926).
President Johnson signs Voting Rights Act, guaranteeing voting rights for black Americans (1965).
MIT software consultant Tim Berners-Lee invents World Wide Web (1991).

7
IBM introduces first electronic calculator (1944).
Explorer 6 spacecraft transmits first-ever photo from space (1959).
NASA presents evidence of ancient microbial life on Mars (1996).

8
Thomas Edison patents the mimeograph (1876).
Daughters of the American Revolution founded (1890).
Great Train Robbery: thieves steal $7 million from London Royal Mail train (1963).

9
Webster-Ashburton Treaty establishes U.S.-Canada as world's longest nonprotected border (1842).
America drops an atomic bomb on Nagasaki (1945).
President Nixon resigns in wake of Watergate scandal (1974).

10
Transatlantic cable laid between U.S. and England (1866).
America's first electric streetcar system opens in Baltimore (1885).
America's Magellan spacecraft lands on Venus (1990).

AUGUST

11
World's first roller rink opens in Newport, RI (1866).
First prisoners arrive at new high-security penitentiary on Alcatraz Island (1934).
Mall of America, nation's largest retail complex, opens in Minnesota (1992).

12
Chicago incorporated, with a population of 350 (1833).
First giant panda born in captivity, at a Mexican zoo (1980).
IBM releases its first personal computer (1981).

13
Taxicabs begin operating in New York City (1907).
Man o' War loses first and only race in his 1,300-race career (1919).
East Germany begins construction on Berlin Wall (1961).

14
President Franklin Roosevelt signs Social Security Act (1935).
Japan surrenders, ending World War II (1945).
India granted independence by Britain (1947).

15
Panama Canal opens to traffic (1914).
"The Wizard of Oz" premiers in Hollywood (1939).
Woodstock Music and Art Fair opens (1969).

16
Gold discovered in Alaska, setting off Klondike Gold Rush (1896).
First issue of Sports Illustrated published (1954).
Elvis Presley dies (1977).

17
Philadelphia replaces New York as capital of U.S. (1790).
Robert Fulton's steamboat makes maiden voyage (1807).
World's first transatlantic crossing in a hot-air balloon completed (1978).

18
Virginia Dare becomes first English child born on American soil (1587).
American women get right to vote, as 19th Amendment is ratified (1920).
First-ever hair-loss treatment, Minoxidil, approved by FDA (1988).

19
World's first beauty contest held in Belgium (1888).
First Indianapolis 500 auto race (1909).
First All-American Soap Box Derby held, in Ohio (1934).

20
Alaska discovered by Danish navigator Vitus Bering (1741).
Dial telephone patented (1896).
First stainless steel produced, in England (1913).

AUGUST

21 American Bar Association founded (1878).
Hawaii admitted to Union as 50th State (1959).
Globe Theatre reopens in London, 383 years after Shakespeare's original burned down (1996).

22 U.S. wins first America's Cup yacht race (1851).
First Victrola record player manufactured (1906).
Mona Lisa stolen from Louvre Museum in Paris (1911).

23 Slavery abolished in British colonies (1833).
First ship-to-shore wireless message sent, to San Francisco (1889).
Hitler and Stalin sign non-aggression pact (1940).

24 Mt. Vesuvius erupts, burying Pompeii and Herculaneum (79).
First potato chips made, by American chef George Crum (1853).
British troops invade Washington, DC, and burn White House during War of 1812 (1814).

25 Galileo demonstrates first telescope in Venice (1609).
U.S. National Park Service created (1916).
Allied troops liberate Paris after four years of Nazi occupation (1944).

26 America's first public kindergarten opens in St. Louis (1873).
America's first roller coaster opens in New Jersey (1929).
International Hockey Hall of Fame opens in Toronto (1961).

27 Earliest recorded hurricane in U.S. history strikes Jamestown, VA (1667).
First U.S. oil well created accidentally by an engineer sinking a shaft in Titusville, PA (1859).
First "Guinness Book of World Records" published (1955).

28 First telegraph cable laid under English Channel (1850).
United Parcel Service begins service (1907).
Martin Luther King, Jr. delivers "I Have a Dream" speech in Washington, DC (1963).

29 First Native-American reservation established (1758).
German airship Graf Zeppelin completes around-the-world flight (1929).
Edwin Land patents Polaroid instant photography (1946).

30 European leaders outlaw crossbow, intending to end war forever (1146).
First prizefight using boxing gloves, won by Jack Dempsey (1884).
"Hot Line" between Washington and Moscow activated to prevent nuclear crises (1963).

31 First U.S. tennis championships played in Newport, RI (1881).
U.S. Census Bureau established (1954).
Princess Diana dies in auto accident in Paris (1997).

SEPTEMBER

1
World's first yacht race, pitting King Charles against brother James, held (1661).
Germany invades Poland, starting WWII (1939).
United Nation's World Health Organization formed (1948).

2
U.S. Treasury Department established (1789).
Vice President Teddy Roosevelt advises, "Speak softly and carry a big stick" (1901).
U.S.-French expedition locates Titanic wreckage (1985).

3
Paris Treaty signed by U.S. and Britain, ending Revolutionary War (1783).
New York's first daily newspaper, The Sun, begins publishing (1833).
Wilderness Act signed into law by President Johnson (1964).

4
World's first cafeteria opens, in New York (1885).
Geronimo captured, ending last U.S.-Indian war (1886).
George Eastman patents first roll-film camera and registers name "Kodak" (1888).

5
Tsar Peter I imposes tax on beards, to reduce Asiatic influences in Russia (1698).
First "Jerry Lewis Labor Day Telethon" to benefit muscular dystrophy airs (1966).
World's longest auto tunnel, St. Gotthard in Swiss Alps, opens (1980).

6
Ferdinand Magellan becomes first person to circle globe (1522).
Mattel sells first Barbie Doll (1959).
"Star Trek" premiers on NBC (1966).

7
Pro Football Hall of Fame opens in Canton, OH (1963).
Drury Gallagher swims around Manhattan in record time of six hours, 41.5 minutes (1983).
Desmond Tutu becomes head of South African Anglican Church (1986).

8
"Pledge of Allegiance" written to honor 400th anniversary of Columbus discovering America (1892).
Frank Sinatra makes radio debut, as member of The Hoboken Four (1935).
President Ford grants pardon to former President Nixon (1974).

9
Elvis Presley makes first appearance on "The Ed Sullivan Show" (1956).
Prisoners riot at maximum-security Attica Correctional Facility near Buffalo, NY (1971).
Princess Grace of Monaco dies in auto accident (1982).

10
Elias Howe patents sewing machine (1846).
Swanson sells first TV dinner (1953).
Picasso's "Guernica" returns to Spain after 40 years, celebrating new democracy (1981).

SEPTEMBER

11
First TV broadcast of Miss America pageant (1954).
President Roosevelt dedicates Boulder Dam (now Hoover Dam) (1936).
And, of course, what we all remember (2001).

12
Henry Hudson discovers Manhattan and Hudson River (1609).
Jacqueline Bouvier marries John F. Kennedy (1953).
World's first Internet browser released by Netscape (1994).

13
New York City becomes U.S capital (1788).
U.S. government takes out first loan, borrowing from Bank of North America (1789).
General Motors introduces first American diesel car, Oldsmobile 88 (1977).

14
British Empire adopts Gregorian calendar, eliminating 11 days of that year (1752).
Frances Scott Key writes "The Star-Spangled Banner" (1814).
America's first department store opened by Alexander Stewart (1848).

15
Scottish bacteriologist Alexander Fleming discovers penicillin (1928).
Environmentalists establish Greenpeace to protest nuclear testing in Alaska (1971).
First issue of USA Today published (1982).

16
Mayflower sets sail from England for New World (1620).
General Motors founded (1908).
American Legion incorporated by Congress (1919).

17
City of Boston incorporated (1630).
U.S. Constitution signed in Philadelphia (1787).
"MASH" premiers on CBS (1972).

18
First issue of The New York Times published (1851).
Jimi Hendrix dies in London at age 27 (1970).
Kidnapped publishing heiress Patricia Hearst rescued in San Francisco (1975).

19
George Washington delivers farewell address as president (1796).
"Mary Tyler Moore Show" premieres on CBS (1970).
New Zealand becomes first nation to grant all women right to vote (1893).

20
Magellen embarks on first around-the-world voyage (1519).
First Cannes Film Festival opens (1946).
Cal Ripkin Jr. plays 2,632nd consecutive major-league baseball game, setting new record (1998).

SEPTEMBER

21
America's first daily newspaper, Penns Packet & General Advertiser, begins publishing (1784).
New York Sun tells 8-year-old Virginia O'Hanlon, "Yes, Virginia, there is a Santa Claus" (1897).
People's Republic of China proclaimed (1949).

22
Nathan Hale executed as a spy by British (1776).
President Lincoln's Emancipation Proclamation declares U.S. slaves "forever free" (1862).
Dead Sea Scrolls made public by California University (1991).

23
America's first baseball team, New York Knickerbockers, organizes (1845).
Keystone Kops created at Mack Sennett's Keystone Studio (1912).
Richard Nixon makes his "Checkers" speech (1952).

24
Prophet Muhammad flees Mecca to escape persecution, starting the Muslim calendar (622).
Babe Ruth plays his last game in Yankee Stadium (1934).
"60 Minutes," TV's longest-running newsmagazine, premieres on CBS (1968).

25
America's first printing press goes into use (1639).
First atomic-powered aircraft carrier, U.S.S. Enterprise, launched (1960).
Sandra Day O'Connor becomes first woman on Supreme Court (1981).

26
Thomas Jefferson appointed first U.S. Sec'y of State, Ed Randolph first Att'y General (1789).
"West Side Story" opens on Broadway (1957).
First televised presidential-election debate, between Kennedy and Nixon (1960).

27
Queen Elizabeth launches as passenger ship at Glasgow (1938).
"Tonight Show" premieres on NBC (1954).
Treasury Sec'y Robert Rubin redesigns U.S. currency for security purposes (1995).

28
Explorer Juan Rodriguez Cabrillo discovers California (1542).
Toronto becomes capital of Canada (1867).
Two U.S. Army planes complete first around-the-world flight (1924).

29
Scotland Yard established in London (1829).
New Haven Railroad launches America's first passenger-train service (1849).
Washington National Cathedral completed after 83 years (1990).

30
World's first book, Johann Gutenberg's Bible, published (1455).
Nazi leaders found guilty of war crimes at Nuremberg trials (1946).
"The Flintstones" premieres on ABC (1960).

OCTOBER

1
Henry Ford introduces Model T (1908).
"The Honeymooners" premieres on CBS (1955).
Walt Disney World opens in Orlando (1971).

2
Philadelphia Mint produces America's first coin: a silver half-dime (1792).
"The Twilight Zone" premieres on CBS (1959).
Thurgood Marshall becomes first black Supreme Court justice (1967).

3
First facsimile photo sent over telephone lines, in Washington, DC (1922).
"The Dick Van Dyke Show" premieres on CBS (1961).
Watergate trial begins (1974).

4
Orient Express makes first run (1883).
First satellite, Sputnik I, launched by U.S.S.R. (1957).
Janis Joplin dies in L.A. at age 27 (1970).

5
Harry Truman becomes first president to make a TV address from White House (1947).
American David Kunst becomes first man to walk around the world (1974).
Dalai Lama awarded Nobel Peace Prize for efforts to free Tibet from China (1989).

6
America's first train robbery committed by Reno brothers, who steal $10,000 (1866).
First full-length talking movie, "The Jazz Singer," premieres in New York (1927).
Pope John Paul II becomes first pontiff to visit White House (1979).

7
Henry Ford introduces the assembly line (1913).
First infrared photograph taken, in Rochester, NY (1931).
U.S. House subcommittee begins investigating rigged TV quiz shows (1959).

8
Great Chicago Fire sparked, when Mrs. O'Leary's cow kicks over a lantern (1871).
Dow Jones begins reporting Dow Jones industrial average (1896).
Brooklyn Dodgers move to L.A. (1957).

9
Leif Ericson becomes first explorer to land in North America (1000).
Yale University chartered in New Haven, CT (1701).
First electric blanket goes on sale in Virginia (1946).

10
Billiard ball patented (1865).
"Dr. No," the first James Bond film, opens (1962).
Panama assumes sovereignty over Canal Zone (1979).

OCTOBER

11
Alaska Davidson becomes first female FBI agent (1922).
First manned Apollo mission, Apollo 7, launched (1968).
"Saturday Night Live" premieres on NBC (1975).

12
Christopher Columbus lands in Bahamas, discovering America (1492).
Rembrandt completes painting of his most famous work, "The Night Watch" (1642).
First transatlantic flight of a dirigible, by Germany's Z3 Zeppelin (1924).

13
George Washington lays White House cornerstone (1792).
Boston Red Sox win first World Series (1903).
Mark Antony arrives in Egypt to consummate affair with queen Cleopatra (48 BC).

14
Martin Luther King Jr. wins Nobel Peace Prize (1964).
First live telecast from manned U.S. spacecraft, Apollo 7 (1968).
6,000 Unification Church couples wed simultaneously in Korea (1982).

15
Edison Electric Light Company incorporated (1878).
Reverend Billy Graham begins his ministry (1949).
"I Love Lucy" debuts on CBS (1951).

16
America's first birth-control clinic opens in Brooklyn, NY (1916).
America's first modern hotel, The Tremont, opens in Boston (1829).
Ten Nazi leaders hanged as war criminals after Nuremberg trials (1946).

17
First issue of National Geographic magazine published (1888).
Mother Teresa of India awarded Nobel Peace Prize (1979).
World's tallest building, 106-story skyscraper in Taiwan, completed (2003).

18
"Cock tail" invented in New York City bar (1776).
U.S. officially takes control of Puerto Rico (1898).
Grand Ole Opry, U.S.'s oldest continuing radio show, debuts on Nashville's WSM Radio (1925).

19
World's largest gold nugget found in New South Wales (1872).
Martin Luther King Jr. arrested at an Atlanta sit-in (1960).
Dow plunges 508 points, a greater percentage decline than Crash of 1929 (1987).

20
49th parallel established as the border between the U.S. and Canada (1818).
Hippodrome opens in NYC as new home of PT Barnum's "Greatest Show on Earth" (1873).
General MacArthur wades ashore in Philippines, fulfilling promise to return after being forced to flee (1944).

OCTOBER

21
Thomas Edison invents light bulb (1897).
Frank Lloyd Wright's Guggenheim Museum opens in Manhattan (1959).
New York Yankees win their 24th World Series (1998).

22
America's first horse show held in New York's Madison Square Garden (1883).
First Xerox copy made (1938).
John Paul II inaugurated as first non-Italian pope in 455 years (1978).

23
Blanche Scott becomes first female aviator, flying 12 feet over Ft. Wayne, IN (1910).
Earliest life (34-billion-year-old fossils) found by U.S. paleontologist Elso Barghoorn (1977).
U.S. national debt tops $1 trillion (1981).

24
World's first soccer team founded in England (1857).
"Take Me Out to the Ball Game" tops the charts (1908).
U.S. blockades Cuba during missile crisis (1962).

25
Tappan introduces microwave oven (1955).
John Steinbeck wins Nobel Prize for Literature (1962).
U.S. invades Grenada (1983).

26
Erie Canal, connecting Lake Erie to New York City, opens (1825).
First use of "getaway car," after a shop hold-up in Paris (1901).
First U.S. savings bonds go on sale (1941).

27
R.H. Macy & Co. opens first store, in Manhattan (1858).
Nylon introduced by DuPont (1938).
Dow drops 554.24 points, largest-ever point decline (1997).

28
America's oldest university, Harvard, founded (1636).
Statue of Liberty dedicated by President Cleveland (1886).
First use of fingerprints in criminal investigations, by St. Louis police (1904).

29
International Red Cross formed by 16 countries meeting in Geneva (1863).
Black Tuesday: Panic-selling on Wall Street ushers in Great Depression (1929).
Senator John Glenn, 77, returns to space after 36 years (1998).

30
Ballpoint pen patented, but will not become commercially available for 57 years (1888).
Orson Welles' "War of the Worlds" broadcast convinces many that Martians have landed (1938).
Dr. Albert Schweitzer wins Nobel Peace Prize (1953).

31
Martin Luther begins Protestant Reformation in Germany (1517).
Mount Rushmore completed after 14 years of work (1941).
American admiral G.J. Dufek becomes first person to land an airplane at South Pole (1956).

NOVEMBER

1
Michelangelo's Sistine Chapel paintings exhibited for first time (1512).
Seabiscuit beats War Admiral in race at Pimlico (1938).
Microsoft releases Windows 1.01 (1985).

2
World's largest airplane, Howard Hughes' Spruce Goose, makes first and only flight (1947).
Chicago Tribune reports Thomas Dewey "defeats" Harry Truman for president (1948).
First commercial radio station, KDKA in Pittsburgh, goes on air (1920).

3
America's first automobile show opens at New York's Madison Square Garden (1900).
First brassiere patented (1914).
Clarence Birdseye first markets his frozen peas (1952).

4
Abraham Lincoln marries Mary Todd (1842).
America's first air-conditioned car, a Packard, exhibited in Chicago (1939).
Vogue stages America's first fashion show, "Fashion Fete," in New York (1914).

5
Parker Brothers introduces game of Monopoly (1935).
John F. Kennedy elected to U.S. House of Representatives (1946).
First black congresswoman, Shirley Chisholm, elected (1968).

6
Jefferson Davis elected to six-year term as Confederate president (1861).
Bolshevik Revolution begins in Russia (1917).
"Meet the Press" debuts on local Washington, DC, TV (1947).

7
Lewis and Clark reach Pacific Ocean (1805).
Cartoon depicting elephant as symbol of Republican Party first appears (1874).
Franklin Roosevelt wins unprecedented fourth term as president (1944).

8
First bourbon whiskey distilled from corn, in Bourbon, KY (1789).
Louvre Museum opens in Paris (1793).
Ronald Reagan elected Governor of California (1966).

9
First issues of The Atlantic Monthly (1857) and Rolling Stone (1967) magazines published.
Giant panda first found in China (1927).
East Germany opens Berlin Wall (1989).

10
U.S. Marine Corps. established by Continental Congress (1775).
U.S. reporter Henry Stanley finds British explorer David Livingstone in central Africa (1871).
"Sesame Street" premieres on PBS (1969).

NOVEMBER

11
World War I ends (1918).
First VCR shown to the public (1965).
World's first computer virus demonstrated at MIT (1983).

12
Harvard chemist Theodore Richards becomes first American awarded a Nobel Prize (1915).
Walt Disney releases "Fantasia" (1940).
America's first drive-up bank window opens in Chicago (1946).

13
Ben Franklin writes, "Nothing is certain but death and taxes" (1789).
"The Sheik" starring Rudolph Valentino released (1921).
Vietnam Veterans Memorial in Washington, DC, dedicated (1982).

14
Herman Melville's "Moby Dick" published (1851).
Niagara Falls power plant begins operation (1896).
Dow closes above 1000 for first time (1972).

15
General Sherman burns Atlanta during Civil War (1864).
League of Nations meets for first time, in Geneva (1920).
First Elvis Presley film, "Love Me Tender," premieres (1956).

16
Suez Canal opens to traffic (1869).
U.S. Federal Reserve System inaugurated (1914).
First postage meter used in lieu of postage stamps (1920).

17
U.S. Congress convenes for first time in new capital: Washington, DC (1800).
First synthetic diamonds unveiled by De Beers of South Africa (1959).
U.S. House of Representatives approves North American Free Trade Agreement (1993).

18
William Tell shoots an apple off his son's head (1307).
America's first ticker-tape parade welcomes Prince of Wales to New York (1919).
Mickey Mouse introduced in Disney's "Steamboat Willie" (1928).

19
President Lincoln delivers Gettysburg Address (1863).
President Reagan meets Soviet leader Mikhail Gorbachev for first time (1985).
First surviving septuplets born to Bobbi McCaughey of Iowa (1997).

20
Nazi leaders put on trial in Nuremberg, Germany (1945).
Britain's Princess Elizabeth marries Duke Philip Mountbatten (1947).
Brazilian soccer star Pelé scores 1,000th goal (1969).

NOVEMBER

21
World's longest suspension bridge, Verrazano Narrows, opens in New York (1964).
First flight of the Concorde, from London to New York (1977).
Declaration ending The Cold War signed in Paris (1990).

22
Pirate Blackbeard killed off coast of North Carolina (1718).
President Kennedy assassinated in Dallas (1963).
Largest-ever swearing-in ceremony, as 38,648 immigrants become U.S. citizens (1985).

23
World's first jukebox installed in San Francisco saloon (1889).
WWII food rationing ends in U.S. (1945).
Vatican abolishes Latin as official language of Catholic mass (1964).

24
Charles Darwin publishes "On the Origin of Species" (1859).
First Air Force One christened (1954).
Jack Ruby shoots Lee Harvey Oswald on live TV (1963).

25
"Hollywood Ten," who refused to testify to Un-American Activities Committee, fired (1947).
Agatha Christie's "Mousetrap," longest-running play of all time, opens in London (1952).
Viking 1 radio signal from Mars proves Einstein's Theory of Relativity (1976).

26
America's first streetcar railway begins service, in New York (1832).
Archaeologists enter King Tut's tomb (1922).
"Casablanca" premieres in New York (1942).

27
Alfred Nobel establishes Nobel Prize (1895).
New York's Penn Station opens as world's largest railway terminal (1910).
First Honda factory in America opens (1948).

28
William Shakespeare marries Anne Hathaway (1582).
America's first automobile race held in Chicago, at top speed of 70 mph (1895).
U.S. spacecraft "Mariner 4" completes first successful mission to Mars (1964).

29
First Italian opera produced in U.S., "The Barber of Seville," opens in New York (1825).
Navy defeats Army 24-0 in first Army-Navy football game, at West Point, NY (1890).
The name "Micro-soft" used by company founder Bill Gates for first time (1975).

30
Egyptian queen Cleopatra dies from poisonous snakebite (30 BC).
First Folies Bergère review staged in Paris (1886).
First Mr. America bodybuilding contest held, at New York World's Fair (1940).

DECEMBER

1
Emperor Napoleon marries Josephine of Martinique (1804).
Game of bingo invented (1929).
First map of human chromosome announced (1999).

2
Napoleon crowned emperor of France (1804).
President James Monroe issues Monroe Doctrine (1823).
Gillette begins selling safety razors (1901).

3
Potatoes introduced in England, from Colombia (1586).
America's first co-educational college, Oberlin, opens in Ohio (1833).
U.S. Army's first female officer sworn in (1948).

4
Senate approves U.S. participation in United Nations (1945).
America's Pioneer Venus 1 goes into orbit around Venus (1978).
Journalist Terry Anderson, last American hostage in Lebanon, freed after 2,455 days (1991).

5
President Polk confirms discovery of gold in California, fanning gold rush (1848).
America's first nudist organization, League for Physical Culture, formed in NYC (1929).
Prohibition ends with repeal of 18th Amendment (1933).

6
First edition of Encyclopedia Britannica published in Scotland (1768).
First edition of The Washington Post published (1877).
California's Orange County files for bankruptcy (1994).

7
Delaware becomes first state in the United States (1787).
America's oldest symphony orchestra, New York Philharmonic, gives first concert (1842).
Japanese bomb Pearl Harbor, and America enters WWII (1941).

8
Pope Pius IX proclaims Immaculate Conception, making Mary free of Original Sin (1854).
President Lincoln announces reconstruction plan for South (1863).
John Lennon slain in New York City (1980).

9
U.S. War Department installs its first computing device (1888).
First U.S. monoplane flown, in Long Island, NY (1909).
Last Studebaker car rolls off assembly line, in South Bend, IN (1963).

10
10,000,000th model T Ford assembled (1915).
First issue of Playboy magazine published (1953).
First planet outside our solar system discovered (1984).

DECEMBER

11
Anesthetic first used during a tooth extraction, in Connecticut (1844).
A Mafia gang steals $5.8 million in cash and jewelry from New York's JFK Airport (1978).
General Electric acquires RCA and its television subsidiary, NBC (1985).

12
Mona Lisa recovered two years after being stolen from the Louvre in Paris (1913).
Arthur Ashe becomes first black person ranked No. 1 in tennis (1968).
Joe Namath plays his last game as a New York Jet (1976).

13
Woodrow Wilson visits France, becoming first president to go overseas while in office (1918).
James Dean makes his acting debut – in a Pepsi commercial (1950).
U.S. forces capture Iraqi dictator Saddam Hussein in Tikrit (2003).

14
World's first table-tennis tournament held in London (1901).
Norwegian explorer Roald Amundsen becomes first person to reach South Pole (1911).
"Saturday Night Fever" premieres in New York, launching disco era (1977).

15
Bill of Rights, containing first 10 amendments to the Constitution, ratified (1791).
Basketball invented by Canadian James Naismith (1891).
"Gone With the Wind" premieres in Atlanta (1939).

16
Boston Tea Party: Patriots dump tea in harbor to protest taxation without representation (1773).
Albert Einstein publishes "General Theory of Relativity" (1915).
Pilot Chuck Yeager becomes first person to break sound barrier (1953).

17
Orville and Wilbur Wright make first powered airplane flight (1903).
U.S. Air Force closes Project Blue Book, stating no evidence exists of UFO sightings (1969).
Budweiser Rocket car breaks sound barrier at 739.7 mph in California (1979).

18
Mother Goose nursery rhymes published (1719).
First photograph of moon shot through a telescope (1849).
Slavery abolished in America (1865).

19
Ben Franklin begins publishing "Poor Richard's Almanack" (1732).
Robert Ripley begins his "Believe It or Not" column, in The New York Globe (1918).
"Titanic," highest-grossing movie of all time, premieres (1997).

20
U.S. buys Louisiana from France for $27 million (1803).
Missouri enacts law to tax bachelors $1 a year (1820).
New York's Broadway first lit by electricity, inspiring nickname "Great White Way" (1880).

DECEMBER

21 Mayflower lands at Plymouth Rock (1620).
Disney's first full-length cartoon, "Snow White and the Seven Dwarfs," premieres (1937).
First crossword puzzle published, in the New York World (1913).

22 World's first Christmas-tree lights created by Thomas Edison (1882).
First ringside radio broadcast of a prizefight, from NYC's Madison Square Garden (1920).
"Dr. Zhivago" premieres (1965).

23 Mayflower Pilgrims begin construction of first permanent settlement in New England (1620).
Clement Moore's "The Night Before Christmas" published (1823).
Sarah Breedlove becomes world's first self-made millionairess (1867).

24 World's first automobile, three-wheeled "steam-wagon," first driven in England (1801).
Enrico Caruso gives last public performance, in New York City (1920).
Apollo 8 becomes first manned spacecraft to orbit moon (1968).

25 Saint Francis of Assisi assembles first-ever Nativity scene (1223).
Halley's Comet first sighted (1758).
Mikhail Gorbachev resigns as Soviet president, marking end of U.S.S.R. (1991).

26 George Washington crosses the Delaware River, defeating 1,400 Hessians (1776).
Flamingo Hotel opens, kicking off an era of glamorous vice in Las Vegas (1946).
America celebrates Kwanzaa for first time (1966).

27 Charles Darwin sets out on Pacific voyage to develop his theories on evolution (1831).
Radio City Music Hall, world's largest indoor theatre, opens in New York (1932).
World Bank created by an agreement signed by 28 nations (1945).

28 Westminster Abbey opens in London (1065).
Dry-cleaning invented (1849).
World's first movie theater opens in Paris (1895).

29 President James Polk turns on White House's first gaslights (1848).
First YMCA opens in Boston (1851).
U.S. Cavalry massacres 200 Native Americans at Wounded Knee Creek, SD (1890)

30 Astronomer Edwin Hubble announces existence of other galactic systems (1924).
Frank Sinatra opens at NYC's Paramount Theatre, launching era of pop-music hysteria (1942).
"Let's Make A Deal" premieres on NBC (1963).

31 General Motors becomes first U.S. corporation to earn $1 billion in single year (1955).
U.S.S.R. dissolved (1991).
U.S. turns over Panama Canal to Panama (1999).

～ Congratulations ～

WE NEVER THOUGHT YOU WOULD

GET THIS FAR...

A. BACALL

"Oh, dear! We are not invited to Harry's hot-tub birthday party. They don't think we will fit in."

"I know I was speeding, officer. I don't want to be late for my surprise birthday party."

"It can't be your birthday again.
You've already had seven this year."

177 LAUGHS GUARANTEED

We guarantee that you will have at least 177 laughs reading this book. To make a claim under this guarantee, you must submit a video showing you reading the entire book and not achieving the guaranteed 177 laughs. In the absence of such a video, you must provide sworn affidavits from a minimum of ten people who were present while the book was being read. The ten affidavits must include at least two justices of the United States Supreme Court.

The total amount of a claim under this guarantee is limited to $1.20, payable in 12 annual installments. All claims shall be subject to a shipping and handling charge of $42.75.

This guarantee is null and void in states where prohibited by law and in any state having a Republican governor.

What are you looking for, an index?

SEE THE NEXT PAGE

.

BUY ANOTHER COPY,
YOU MAY FIND IT THERE!